D1535493

THE PSYCHOANALYTICAL

TREATMENT OF CHILDREN

THE PSYCHOANALYTICAL
TREATMENT OF CHILDREN

Lectures and Essays

by ANNA FREUD

Schocken Books • New York

Parts I and II were translated from the
German by Nancy Proctor-Gregg.

First SCHOCKEN PAPERBACK edition 1964

Third Printing, 1969

Translator's Note

For members of the teaching profession and parents who may have no particular knowledge of psychoanalysis and its terminology, I venture to proffer here some very rough-and-ready explanations of the more technical terms, which are naturally used without elucidation in lectures addressed directly to practising analysts, but which might prove a stumbling block to a wider circle of readers.

It will be appreciated that such explanations are strictly *ad hoc*, directed merely to the purpose of making this book more intelligible to the lay reader. No criticism of the conceptions embodied in the terms explained can justly be founded on them; brief notes of this kind upon the terminology of a young science cannot be framed in such a way as to stand examination directed to the premises of the science itself.

I assume that the conception of *"the unconscious"* is nowadays fairly clear to most people. It is that highly active self within us of which *ex hypothesi* we are not directly aware. We are, of course, always aware of some (not all) of its activities, even in sleep, when we dream. *Repression* is the process applied to impulses, notions, etc. unwelcome to our conscious selves, which we mean to, but cannot, discard; repression throws them, not into the discard (as we may have supposed until the analytical undoing of repression in the treatment of some consequential neurosis leads to their reappearance), but into the unconscious. Repression in this technical sense, i.e. "making unconscious," is naturally itself an unconscious process (though the movement towards rejection may not have been) and permits no memory of the occasion.

The *Id,* the *Ego* and the *Super-ego* are terms which to be properly understood, so far as understanding yet goes, require at least a book to themselves. They may very broadly be thought of, for the purpose of understanding these lectures, as respectively the unconscious, the conscious, and the "conscience" functions of the self. Both Ego and Super-ego dip deep into the unconscious, and should not be thought of as by any means entirely accessible to awareness. It is part of the theory of the Super-ego that it is the *internal* judge of the self, which has developed, largely unconsciously, from the "internalisation" of requirements and ideals to which the self at some period has given allegiance: usually those adumbrated by the parents, whether consciously or merely in the child's—often distorting—imagination.

The *"transference"* is the very emotional attitude assumed by the patient, under the direction of his unconscious, in analysis towards the analyst; arising, very roughly speaking, from the fact that the analyst who re-elicits repressed reactions becomes the representative of what originally occasioned either them or their repression.

The meaning of the other technical terms used will probably be deduced from their nomenclature or context. *"Compulsion-neurosis"* is of course the common kind of mental maladjustment which so often takes a mild form in people who feel they cannot (or must) step on the cracks in the pavement. The *latency period* is that beginning usually about the fifth year of a child's life and lasting until puberty; the child's early active and highly varied sexual impulses, connected with the various "erogenous zones" of the body affording gratification (ranging from the pleasures of sucking to those of anal activity, onanism, etc.), become largely latent; the energy supplying them is to a great extent diverted.

The *Oedipus complex,* to which so many sinister allusions are made by those who do not trouble or do not like to inform themselves of what they are talking about, is merely a handy, almost algebraical, way of denoting the whole set of feelings attached to the natural impulse of all children to crave for exclusive love, usually from the parent of the opposite sex. The myth of Oedipus, who *unknowingly* carried the fulfilment of this instinct to its extreme, by killing his father and marrying his mother, stands conveniently for the whole complex of this wish, and its derivatives; which may (like any other desire which the individual may be unable to handle satisfactorily) lead to unhappy consequences when repressed into the unconscious.

As for the function of *analysis* itself, a brilliant short exposition will be found in the fourth lecture (p. 47), in a passage which may be read with profit before the book is begun.

Table of Contents

Preface

Part I of this series comprises a course of lectures given in 1926 before the Vienna Institute of Psycho-Analysis under the title *Introduction to the Technique of the Psycho-Analysis of Children* (1). Part II, which slightly amplifies the subject matter treated in this introductory series of lectures, was, soon afterwards, read as a paper at the Tenth International Psycho-Analytical Congress in Innsbruck, 1927 (2). Part III was written for *The Psychoanalytic Study of the Child*, 1945 (3), and attempts to summarise some of the advances in the understanding and evaluation of the infantile neurosis which the author has made in the intervening nineteen years of work on the subject.

The audience of the first five lectures was, in each instance, composed of practising and prospective analysts, and accordingly both subject and phraseology of the main part of the book are technical.

It is not the author's fault that the early material contained in this publication is presented to the English reader at such a late date. An English version of the *Introduction to the Technique of Child-Analysis* (4) was published in America. Attempts at publication in England were not successful. For the general publisher the subject matter was still too remote and controversial. Professional psychoanalytical circles in England, on the other hand, were at that time concentrating their interest on Mrs. Melanie Klein's new theory and technique of the analysis of children (5). The British Psycho-Analytical Society devoted a *Symposion on Child-Analysis* (6) to a severe criticism of the author's efforts, which ran counter to Mrs. Klein's outlook. The *Introduction to the Technique of the Analysis of Children* was rejected when offered to The International Psycho-Analytical Library for publication, and the matter lapsed, so far as England was concerned.

In Vienna, from 1927 onward, a group of analysts, later joined by colleagues from Budapest and Prague, held regular meetings with the author to discuss the technique of the analysis of children, as it emerged from these introductory lectures, to report on cases which were treated with this method, to compare results, and to clarify the theoretical background of the practical findings. The age range to which the technique was found applicable was lowered from the latency period, as originally suggested, to two years, and extended at the other end to pre-adolescence and adolescence. All types of non-organic disturbances of childhood development were taken into treatment, from the usual phobias, hysterical illnesses, obsessional disturbances, bed-wetting, stammering, compulsive masturbation and exhibitionism, neurotic constipation, to grave abnormalities of a schizophrenic type (7-30). Analyses of delinquent children were attempted and carried out, in close co-operation with the work of August Aichhorn on juvenile delinquency which was developed and taught by him in Vienna at the same time (31-34).

Before these developments in the field of analytical therapy for children, Vienna had already been a fertile ground for the psychoanalytical study of normal child development, and for the application of this new knowledge to education. Students of the subject had for years been listening to the inspiring lectures for teachers and youth leaders given by Siegfried Bernfeld (39-42), and many young and enthusiastic workers had taken part in his experiment in education in "Kinderheim Baumgarten," a camp school for homeless children which formed part of the American relief work for children in the

post-war period after 1918. In 1929 the author was commissioned by the School Inspectorate of the City of
Vienna to give four lectures on psychoanalysis to the
teachers of the Children's Centres of the City (50). This
marked a further step in the co-operation between psychoanalysis and education, which from then onward developed freely in all its branches. Some members of the
Vienna Institute of Psycho-Analysis devoted a fair share
of their teaching and lecturing activity to consolidating
the ground which had been gained. The Vienna Psycho-
Analytic Society thus (besides training for the therapeutic analysis of neurotic and delinquent children) spon-
sored one Child Guidance Clinic for young children (directed by Edith Sterba), one Child Guidance Clinic for
adolescents (directly by August Aichhorn); special discussion groups for teachers of the city who dealt with
problem children in their own classrooms; and, organised by Dr. W. Hoffer, a three year post graduate
Training Course for teachers who received instruction
in psychoanalytical child psychology, and guidance in its
application to their handling of children (35-38, 43-68).
To these ventures was added in 1937 an experimental
Day-Nursery for infants between one and two years of
age, which was founded and maintained by Dr. Edith
Jackson, New Haven, and organised by the author in
conjunction with Mrs. Dorothy Burlingham, and with
the medical help of Dr. Josefine Stross.

So far as Vienna was concerned, these activities ended
with the political changes in 1938. Nearly all the par-
ticipants in the work left Austria, to continue elsewhere.
Both sides of the work, the therapeutic as well as the one
applied to education, were pursued further in the new
surroundings. Members of the former Vienna Seminars
for Children's Analysis joined up, in Holland or America, with other analytic colleagues to form similar seminars and discussion groups, or, as in England, continued

the work among themselves. Analytic Child Study and work with educators was welcomed in all countries, for in the meantime interest in the problems of upbringing of normal and abnormal children had gradually increased. Experimental Nurseries based on analytic principles came into being in Boston, Detroit and Los Angeles. The organisers of the Vienna Nursery, now in London, founded and directed the so-called Hampstead Nurseries (69, 70), a Residential War Nursery, financed by the Foster Parents' Plan for War Children, Inc., New York, to which a three years' theoretical and practical Training Course for Children's Nurses and Teachers was attached.

The extensive work done in psychoanalysis applied to education had in time its welcome repercussions on the therapeutic analysis of children, and led to important modifications on the technical side. In 1926, before there was any systematic teaching of either parents, teachers, or children's nurses, the author was justified in saying that the children's analyst must "claim for himself liberty to guide the child . . ." (p. 53) and "accordingly combine in his own person two difficult and diametrically opposed functions: he has to analyse and educate, . . ." (p. 59). In 1946, after twenty years of intervening work with educators, such a statement is no longer legitimate. The children's analyst now shares his knowledge of the child's requirements with the workers in the field of education and upbringing, and accordingly his task has become easier. Whereas formerly he himself had to assume the "position of authority" (p. 54), he can now, with rare exceptions, concentrate his energies on the purely analytic side of the task, and count on the co-operation of enlightened parents, school teachers or nurses to supply the intelligent control and guidance of the child which are the indispensable accompaniment and counterpart of its analysis.

For reasons of another kind, certain statements made in the First Lecture on *An Introductory Phase in the Analysis of Children*, must be modified in the light of modern developments. In a study of the defence mechanisms of the ego (7), the author described ways and means to uncover and penetrate the first resistances in the analysis of children, whereby the introductory phase of the treatment is shortened and, in some instances, rendered unnecessary. Berta Bornstein, in a recent publication (72), gives a useful and well illustrated account of the technical changes in the analysis of children which arise from the study of their various defence mechanisms.

The Second Lecture does not require similar modifications. The author's views on *The Methods of Children's Analysis* have to a large degree remained unchanged.

The opinions expressed in the Third Lecture, on *The Role of Transference in the Analysis of Children*, have during the last twenty years been repeatedly opposed by children's analysts in England and America who maintain that the children under their treatment show profuse signs of transference which is open to analysis in the same manner as in the analysis of adult patients. The author fully agrees that this is the case. But, in spite of these manifold and variegated transferred reactions of the child, the author has not, so far, met a single case of a child patient where the original neurosis was given up during the treatment and replaced by a new neurotic formation in which the original objects had disappeared and the analyst taken their place in the patient's emotional life. It is only a structure of this kind which deserves the name of transference-neurosis. So far as the author's experience goes, the latter occurs solely in cases of adult neurotics who are treated with the classical technique applicable only to patients who have reached maturity.

PART I

Introduction
to the Technique of
the Analysis of Children
(1926)

FIRST LECTURE

An Introductory Phase in the Analysis of Children

Ladies and Gentlemen. It is difficult to assert anything about the technique of the analysis of children without first making clear one's position on the question: in which cases would one in general consider that an analysis should be undertaken, and in which would it be better to refrain?

Mrs. Melanie Klein has as you know fully considered this question in her publications and in her lectures. She takes the view that any disturbance in the intellectual or other psychological development of a child can be resolved or at least favourably influenced by an analysis. She goes still further, and maintains that an analysis is of the greatest benefit also to the development of a normal child, and in the fulness of time will become indispensable to complete all modern education. On the other hand, it transpired in the course of a discussion at one of our meetings last year that the majority of our Viennese analysts take a different point of view, and maintain that the analysis of a child is only appropriate in the case of an infantile neurosis.

I am afraid that I am not going to be able to contribute much in the course of these lectures to the elucidation of this question. The most I can do is to give you an account of what cases I did undertake to analyse, and say in which of them this decision proved justified and in which the analysis came to grief owing to internal or external difficulties. It is natural that when one comes to make fresh decisions one is encouraged by a recent success and apt to be deterred by a failure. On the whole, I think one sometimes gets the impression in working with children that analysis is here a method too difficult, costly and complicated, that one does too much with it; contrariwise, in other cases, and that still more often, one feels that with pure analysis one accomplishes much too little.

It may thus happen that analysis, where children are concerned, requires special modifications and adjustments, or indeed can only be undertaken subject to certain precautions. Where then the introduction of these precautions is impracticable, the carrying out of an analysis may be inadvisable.

In the course of these lectures you will see from manifold examples the application of the foregoing remarks. I shall on purpose leave for the present on one side any attempt to take this question further, and shall concern myself with the technical process of the analysis of children in those cases where for some reason, which for the moment we shall not go into, it seems advisable to undertake that treatment.

In the last year I have several times been invited to give a report of an analysis of a child at one of the technical courses of our Society, and to examine in that connection the special technique of the analysis of children. Up to now I have always declined this request, for I was afraid that anything that one could say on this subject must seem to you banal and obvious. The special technique of the analysis of children, in so far as it is special at all, derives from one very simple fact: that the adult is—at least to a considerable degree—a mature and independent being, while the child is immature and not self-dependent. It is evident that to deal with such different subjects the method cannot remain uniform. Many of its elements, important and significant in an adult case, lose their importance in the new situation; the rôles of various expedients are shifted, and what was there a necessary and innocuous procedure becomes here perhaps risky. Such modifications however occur to everyone according to circumstances, and hardly require a special theoretical foundation.

In the last two and a half years however I have had the opportunity to conduct ten long analyses of children, and I shall try in what follows to arrange the observations which I was enabled to make in the way in which they would probably have impressed anyone amongst you under equally favourable circumstances.

We shall accordingly keep to the actual sequence of events as they occur in an analysis, and begin with the attitude of the child at the outset of the analytical work.

Let us consider first the analogous situation with an adult patient. A person feels that he is disturbed, in his work or his enjoyment of life, by some sort of difficulty within himself; he gains, on one ground or another, confidence in the therapeutical power of analysis or of some particular analyst; and he makes the decision to seek a remedy by this means. I know of course that the facts are not always altogether like this. It is not always exclusively the inner difficulties which are the motive for the analysis—frequently this is only provided by the conflicts with environment which arise from them. Again, the decision is not always made really independently; pressure from relatives or others often plays a rôle greater than is favourable for the later progress of the work. Nor is confidence in analysis and the analyst always a factor. But still it always remains for the treatment the wished-for and ideal situation, that the patient should of his own free will ally himself with the analyst against a part of his inward being.

This state of things is naturally never to be found amongst children. The decision for analysis never comes from the child who is to be the patient, but always from the parents or other persons round it. The child is not asked for its consent. If the question were put to it, it could hardly pronounce an opinion or find an answer. The analyst is a stranger, analysis itself something unknown.

But what constitutes an even greater difficulty is that in many cases the child itself is not the sufferer, for it often does not perceive the trouble in itself at all; only the persons round it suffer from its symptoms or outbreaks of naughtiness. And so the situation lacks everything which seems indispensable in the case of the adult: insight into the malady, voluntary decision, and the will towards cure.

This does not impress every analyst of children as a serious obstacle. You will be aware from Mrs. Melanie Klein's writings how she comes to terms with these circumstances and what technique she founds on them. To me, on the contrary, it seems that one ought to try whether one cannot produce in the child's case, too, the situation which has proved so favourable in the adult's, that is to say, whether one cannot induce in the child in some way the missing readiness and willingness.

I shall make it the subject of my first lecture to show you how in six different cases, of ages between six and eleven, I succeeded in making the small patient "analysable" in the sense of the adult, that is to say inducing an insight into the trouble, imparting confidence in the analyst, and turning the decision for analysis from one taken by others into its own. Children's analysis requires for this task a preparatory period which does not occur with adults. I must emphasize that everything which we undertake in this period has nothing to do with the real analytical work, that is to say there is as yet no question of making unconscious processes conscious or of analytical influence on the patient. It is simply a matter of converting an unsuitable situation into a desirable one, by

all the means which are at the disposal of an adult dealing with a child. This time of preparation—the "dress-
age" for analysis one might properly call it—will last the
longer, the further the original condition of the child is
from that of the ideal adult patient which has already
been described.

Such a task need not moreover always be very difficult; the step which has to be taken is often not a specially big one. I am reminded of the case of a little six-
year-old who was sent to me last year for three weeks'
observation. I had to determine whether the difficult,
silent and unpleasing nature of the child was due to a
defective disposition and unsatisfactory intellectual development, or whether we had here a case of an especially inhibited and dreamy child. Closer observation revealed the presence of a compulsion neurosis, unusually
severe and well-defined for such an early age, together
with acute intelligence and keen logical powers. In this
case the introductory process proved very simple. The
little girl already knew two children who were being
analysed by me, and she came the first time to the appointment with her slightly older friend. I said nothing
special to her, and merely left her to gain a little confidence in the strange surroundings. The next time, when
I had her alone, I made the first attack. I said that she
knew quite well why her two friends came to me, one
because he could never tell the truth and wanted to give
up this habit, and the other because she cried so often
and was angry with herself for doing so; and I wondered
whether she too had been sent to me for some such reason. At that she said quite frankly "I have a devil in me.
Can it be taken out?"

I was for a moment taken aback at this unexpected
answer. Certainly it could, I said, but it would be no
light work. And if I were to try with her to do it, she

would have to do a lot of things which she would not find at all agreeable. (I meant of course that she would have to tell me everything.)

She had a moment or two of earnest meditation, then she replied, "If you tell me that it is the only way to do it, and to do it quickly, then I shall do it that way." Thereby of her own free will she bound herself by the essential rule of analysis. We ask nothing more of an adult patient at the outset. But further, she fully understood the question of the length of time necessary. When the three weeks were up her parents were undecided whether to leave her under analysis with me or to put her under other care. She herself however was very disquieted, not wanting to give up the hope awakened while with me that she would be cured, and kept insistently demanding that if she had to go I should rid her of her devil in the three or four days remaining. I assured her that this was impossible and that it would take a long time of working together. I could not make this intelligible to her with numbers, for although she was already of school age, on account of her numerous inhibitions she had as yet no knowledge of arithmetic. Thereupon she sat herself down on the floor, pointed at the pattern of my carpet, and said, "Will it take as many days as there are red bits? Or even as many as the green bits?" I showed her the great number of appointments that would be necessary by referring to the many medallions in the pattern. She fully grasped the point, and in the imminent decision did her part in persuading her parents of the necessity for a very long time of working with me.

You may say that in this case it was the gravity of the neurosis which lightened the work of the analyst. But I think that would be a mistake. I will give you an example of another case in which the introductory phase took a similar course, although there could have been no question of a real neurosis at all.

About two and a half years ago I made the analytical acquaintance of a difficult little girl of nearly eleven. She was from the well-to-do Viennese middle-class, but the relationships in her home were unfavourable, for her father was weak and little concerned with her, the mother had been dead for some years, and her relationship with the father's second wife and a younger step-brother was unsatisfactory. A number of thefts by the child, and an unending series of crude lies and small and great concealments and insincerities had determined the stepmother, on the advice of the family physician, to seek the aid of analysis. Here the analytical treaty was equally simple. "Your parents cannot do anything with you," was the basis of the negotiations, "with their help alone you will never get out of the constant scenes and conflicts. Perhaps you will try the help of a stranger." She accepted me without more ado as an ally against her parents, just as the little compulsion-neurotic I described before did against her devil. The insight into the malady of the compulsion-neurotic was here clearly replaced by insight into the conflict; the factor actually common to both however was the amount of suffering, which in the first case sprang from inward causes and in the second from outer.

My next procedure in this second case was throughout that recommended by Aichhorn for the educational treatment of delinquent children. The probation officer entrusted with the care of such children, says Aichhorn, must first of all put himself on the side of the delinquent, and assume that the child is justified in its attitude to those about it. Only so will he succeed in working with his charge instead of against him. I might emphasize here that Aichhorn's position for this kind of work has considerable advantage over that of the analyst. He is authorised to interfere by the state or town, and he has behind him the authority of an official position. The analyst on the contrary, as the child knows, is commissioned and perhaps paid by the parents, and he always gets into an awkward position if he sets himself against his clients, even if it is in their own interest. In fact I never held the necessary consultations with this child's parents without feeling uneasy, and the analysis after some weeks, in spite of the best inherent conditions, finally came to grief on account of this unclarified relationship.

In these two cases at all events the preliminaries necessary for the beginning of a real analysis, the sense of suffering, confidence in analysis and decision in favour of it, were created with little trouble. Let us now go to the other extreme, and consider a case in which none of these three factors was present.

This was a ten-year-old boy with an obscure mixture of many anxieties, nervous states, insincerities and childish perverse habits. Various small and one more serious theft had occurred in recent years. The conflict with his home surroundings was no open and conscious one, and on the surface any insight into his very uncomfortable condition, or any wish to change it, was not to be found. His attitude to me was one of thorough-going rejection and mistrust, his whole endeavour being directed to protecting his sexual secrets from discovery. Here I could not employ either of the two expedients which had proved feasible in the other two cases. I could neither ally myself with his conscious Ego against a split-off part of his nature (for he felt nothing of such a division), nor offer myself as a partner against his surroundings, to which so far as he was consciously aware he was attached by the strongest feelings. I clearly had to take another course, more difficult and less direct, for it was a question of creeping into a confidence which was not to be won directly, and forcing myself upon a person who was of the opinion that he could do very well without me.

I tried to do this in various ways. At first, for a long time, I did nothing but follow his moods and humours along all their paths and bypaths. Did he come to his appointment in a cheerful disposition, I was cheerful too; if he were serious or depressed, I was the same. Did he prefer, instead of moving about or sitting or lying down, to spend the hour under the table, I would treat it as the most natural thing in the world and hold up the tablecloth and speak to him under it. If he came with string in his pocket, and began to show me remarkable knots and tricks, I would let him see that I could make more complicated knots and do more remarkable tricks. If he made faces, I pulled better ones, and if he challenged me to trials of strength I showed myself incomparably stronger. But I followed his lead in every subject of talk, from tales of pirates and questions of geography to stamp-collections and love stories. In these conversations nothing was too grown-up or too delicate a subject for me to talk to him about, and not even his mistrustfulness could suspect an educational intention behind what I said. My way was rather like that of a film or novel which has no other intention than to attract the audience or reader to itself, and with this aim concentrates on the interests and needs of its public. My first aim was in fact nothing else but to make myself interesting to the boy. That in this first period I became familiar at the same time with many of his interests and inclinations which lay near the surface was an accessory advantage.

After a time I brought in another factor. I proved myself useful to him in small ways, wrote letters for him on the typewriter during his visits, was ready to help him with the writing down of his daydreams and self-in-

vented stories of which he was proud, and made all sorts
of little things for him during his hour with me. In the
case of a little girl who was undergoing her preparation
at the same time I zealously crochetted and knitted during her appointments, and gradually clothed all her
dolls and teddy bears.

To put it briefly, I developed in this way a second
agreeable quality—I was not only interesting, I had become useful. As an accessory gain in this second period
I had by means of the letter and story writing obtained
an introduction into the sphere of his acquaintance and
his fantasies.

Then however came something incomparably more
important. I made him notice that being analysed has
very great practical advantages, that for example pun-
ishable deeds have an altogether different and much
more fortunate result when they are first told to the
analyst, and only through him to those in charge of the
child. And thus he got the habit of relying on analysis
as a protection from punishment and claiming my help
for repairing the consequences of his rash acts; he let me
restore stolen money in his place and got me to make all
necessary but disagreeable confessions to his parents.
He tested my abilities in this direction over and over
again before he decided really to believe in them. After
that however there were no more doubts; besides an interesting and useful companion I had become a very
powerful person, without whose help he could no longer
get along. Thus in these three capacities I had made
myself indispensable to him. He was now in full dependence and in a transference relationship. I had however only waited for this moment to require of him in
return—not in terms and not all at one stroke—very
energetic and comprehensive co-operation; namely the
surrender, so necessary for analysis, of all his previously

guarded secrets, which then took up the next weeks and months and with which the real analysis first began.

You observe that in this case I concerned myself not at all with the establishment of insight into the malady, which in later progress came of itself in quite a different way; here the problem was only the creation of a tie between us, which must be strong enough to sustain the later analysis.

But I fear from this detailed description you may think that there was nothing at stake but this tie. I will try to reduce this impression with the help of other examples which hold a middle course between the two extremes I have mentioned.

I was called upon to analyse another ten-year-boy, who had recently developed a symptom which was very unpleasant and disturbing to those about him, namely noisy outbursts of rage and naughtiness, which broke out for no intelligible outward reason and were very strange in this otherwise inhibited and timid child. It was easy in this case to gain his confidence, for I was already known to him. The decision for analysis harmonised too with his own intentions, for his younger sister was already my patient, and jealousy of the advantages of her position in the family which she clearly derived from this fact made his wishes turn in the same direction. In spite of this I found no direct point of attack for the analysis; but the explanation was not far to seek. He had indeed so far as his anxiety was concerned a partial insight into the malady, and a certain desire to get rid of it and of his inhibitions. But for his main symptom, the rages, it was rather the contrary. Of them he was unmistakably proud, regarding them as something which distinguished him from others (if indeed not directly in a favourable sense), and he enjoyed the worry they caused his parents. He thus felt himself in a certain sense at one with this symptom, and would probably at that time have resisted any attempt to rid him of it with analytical help. But here I ambushed him in a not very honest way. I resolved to embroil him with that part of his nature, I made him describe the outbreaks as often as they came and showed myself concerned and thoughtful. I enquired how far in such states he was yet master of his action at all, and compared his fits of rage to those of a madman who would be beyond my aid. At that he was startled and rather frightened, for to be regarded as mad naturally did not chime with his ambitions. He now tried himself to master these outbreaks, began to resist them instead of as earlier to encourage them; thereby he noticed his real lack of strength to suppress them and so felt an enhancement of his feelings of suffering and discomfort. After a few vain attempts the symptom finally, as I had intended, turned from a treasured possession into a disturbing foreign body, to fight which he only too readily claimed my help.

It will strike you that in this case I induced a condition which had been present from the beginning in the little compulsion-neurotic: a split in the child's inner being. In yet another case, of a seven-year-old neurotically naughty little girl, I determined on the same artifice at the end of a long preparatory period similar to those already described. I suddenly separated off all her naughtiness and personified it before her, giving it a name of its own and confronting her with it, and eventually succeeded insofar that she began to complain of the person thus newly created by me, and obtained an insight into the amount of suffering she had endured from it. The "analysability" of the child came hand in hand with the insight into the malady established in this way.

But we must not forget another limitation. I once

analysed an unusually gifted and sensitive little girl who cried too easily. She wanted very much to get over this tendency with the help of analysis. But the work with me always stuck at a certain stage, and I was on the point of contenting myself with a minor amelioration. At that point there emerged clearly as an obstruction a tender attachment to a nurse, who was not friendly towards analysis; and our efforts, as they really came to penetrating the depths, struck upon it. The child indeed believed me as to what emerged from the analysis and what I said, but only up to a certain point—a stage to which she had allowed herself to go and where her loyalty to the nurse began. Whatever went beyond it struck upon a tenacious and unassailable resistance. She regressed in fact to an old conflict in the love-choice between her parents who lived apart, which had played an important rôle in her early childhood development. But this disclosure again did not really help, for the recent attachment to the person of her nurse was a thoroughly real and well-founded one.

Then I began a keen and sustained battle with the nurse for the child's affection, conducted on both sides with every possible expedient; in it I awakened her criticism, tried to shake her blind dependence, and turned to my account every one of the little conflicts which occur daily in a nursery. I knew that I had won, when one day the little girl told me again the story of such an incident which had affected her at home, but this time added "Do you think she's right?" Only from then on could the analysis penetrate the depths, and it led to the most promising result of all the cases I have mentioned.

The decision as to whether this method, the battle for the child itself, is permissible was in this case made without difficulty; the nurse's influence would have been bad not only for the analysis but for the whole development of the child. But consider how impossible such a situation is when one has as an opponent no stranger but the child's parents, or when one is faced with the question of whether it is worth depriving the child, in the interests of a successful analysis, of someone's really favourable and desirable influence. We shall return to this point in more detail when we consider the question of the prospects of the analysis of children and the relationship with the child's environment.

I shall conclude this subject with two more little stories, meant to show you how far the child is able to grasp the meaning of analytical work and of the therapeutical problem.

The best of them comes from the case of the little compulsion-neurotic. She recounted to me one day an unusually well-sustained battle with her devil, and suddenly demanded appreciation. "Anna Freud," she said, "am I not much stronger than my devil? Can't I control him very well by myself? I don't think I need you for it at all." I fully confirmed that. She was really much stronger, and without my help. "But I do need you," she said after pondering for a minute, "you have to help me not to be so unhappy at having to be stronger than it." I think that even from a grown-up neurotic one can expect no better understanding of the change he hopes for from analysis.

And now for the second story. My naughty ten-year-old whom I have already described in detail, in a later period of his analysis got into conversation one day in the waiting room with one of my father's adult patients. This man told him about his dog, which had killed a fowl for which he, the owner, had had to pay. "The dog ought to be sent to Freud," said my little patient, "he needs analysis." The grown-up did not reply, but afterwards showed great disapproval. What odd sort of idea of analysis did the child have? The dog had nothing the matter with it; it wanted to kill the hen and it killed it. I knew exactly what the boy had meant. "The poor dog," he must have thought, "he wants so badly to be a good dog and something inside him forces him to kill hens."

As you see, insight into naughtiness had in the little neurotic delinquent shifted without difficulty into the place of insight into the malady, and thus provided a fully sufficient motive for analysis.

SECOND LECTURE

The Methods of Children's Analysis

Ladies and Gentlemen. I apprehend that my recent account of myself will have left an odd impression upon those among you who are practising analysts. My proceedings altogether, as I presented them to you, contradict at too many points the rules for the technique of psychoanalysis as laid down for us in the past.

Let us review once more the various things I did:

I gave the little girl a positive promise of cure, bearing in mind the consideration that one cannot demand of a child that with one who was previously a stranger it should follow an unknown path to an uncertain end; I fulfilled in this way her apparent desire to be compelled by authority and wrapped in security. I openly offered myself as an ally, and joined the child in criticising its parents.

In another case I embarked on a secret struggle with the home circle, and courted the child's affections in all possible ways.

To achieve my aim I exaggerated the possible gravity of a symptom, and frightened the patient.

And finally I crept into the children's confidence, and obtruded upon individuals who were firmly of the opinion that they could do very well without me.

Where in all this is the delicate restraint prescribed for the analyst; the prudence with which one holds out to the patient an uncertain prospect of the possibility of cure, or merely of amelioration; the scrupulous discretion in all personal matters; the absolute frankness in reviewing the malady; and the full freedom which one gives the patient to break off the mutual work whenever he likes of his own accord?

I must defend myself against the suspicion which has perhaps arisen in you, that I proceeded as I did in ignorance or unintentional neglect of the prescribed rules. I maintain that I simply elaborated, to suit a new situation, the elements of an attitude which without stressing it particularly you all adopt in dealing with your patients.

Perhaps in my first lecture I exaggerated the difference between the child's initial situation and that of the adult. You know how insecure in the early days of an analysis seem the maintenance of resolution and the patient's confidence. We are in danger of losing him before he has begun the analysis at all, and we only feel that our proceedings are on sure ground when we have him firmly in the transference relation. In these first days however we work upon him, almost imperceptibly and without noticing that we are taking any special pains, in a number of ways which are not so very different from my laborious and apparently distinctive methods with children.

Take for example a melancholic patient. It is true that analytical therapy and technique are not directly designed for such cases, but if one is undertaken a preparatory period of this kind must be inserted, in which the patient's interest and resolution for the analytical work is awakened by the analyst's sympathy and by his entering into his personal needs.

Or take another case. Technical precepts warn us, as you know, against interpreting dreams too early and thereby offering the patient knowledge of his inner processes which he can only reject instead of understanding. But with an intelligent and educated compulsion-neurotic who doubts everything, we may be glad to be able to offer him, at the very outset of the treatment, an especially happy and impressive dream-interpretation. Thereby we interest him and satisfy his exacting intellectual demands—and at bottom we are doing nothing else but what the children's analyst does, when he shows a boy that he can do much cleverer tricks with a piece of string than he can himself.

Another analogy is to be found in the way in which we show ourselves to be on the side of the rebellious and delinquent child and ready to help him against his world. We show the adult neurotic too that we are there to help and support him, and we take his part exclusively in all conflicts with his family; proving ourselves thus to be useful.

Moreover the factor of power and external authority plays a part. Observation shows that the experienced analyst with a reputation finds it much easier to hold his patient and to save him from "absconding" in the early stages than the young beginner; and towards him less "negative transference" and indications of hostility and mistrust are evinced. We ascribe this difference to the young analyst's inexperience, his lack of tact in his demeanour towards the patient, his precipitation or over-caution in interpretation. But I believe that just here one should take into account the factor of external authority. The patient asks himself, not without reason, who this man is after all, who suddenly claims to exercise such prodigious authority over him; and whether his claims are justified by his position in the world and the attitude of other, normal, people towards him. This is not necessarily a matter of the recrudescence of old hostile impulses, but rather perhaps a stirring of critical common sense before the patient lets himself slide into the analytical transference situation. But the eminent analyst with a name and position obviously enjoys, by virtue of the esteem in which he is held, the same advantages as the children's analyst, who in any case is bigger and older than his little patient, and who becomes a person of undoubted power when the child feels that his authority is put by the parents even higher than their own.

Thus these features might be regarded as the elements of an introductory phase of the treatment, such as I have already described, with adults as well as children. But I think I am expressing myself on this incorrectly. It would be more appropriate to say that in the technique of the analysis of adults we find *vestiges* of all the expedients which prove necessary with children. The extent to which we use them will depend upon how far the adult patient with whom we are dealing is still an immature and dependent being, approximating in this respect to a child.

So much for the introductory phase to the treatment, the establishment of the analytical situation. In what follows let us suppose that the child, by all the foregoing means, has really won confidence in the analyst, possesses insight into the malady and is now striving of its own accord for a change in its condition. So we come to our second theme—an examination of the means at our disposal with a child for the analytical work proper.

In the technique of analysis of adults we have four such expedients. We turn to account anything which the patient's conscious memory can furnish for the establishment of as complete a history of his malady as possible; we employ dream interpretation; we assess and interpret the ideas brought up by the patient's free association; and finally through the interpretation of his transference-reactions we obtain access to all those parts of his past life which can be translated into consciousness in no other way. I must inflict upon you in what follows a systematic examination of these expedients in their applicability to and utility for the analysis of children.

In the construction of the case history from the patient's conscious memories we come across the first difference. In adult cases, as you know, we refrain from bringing in any information at all from the patient's family and rely entirely upon what he can tell us himself. This voluntary restriction is based on the fact that communications imparted by the relatives are apt to be unreliable and incomplete, and take their colour from the relatives' personal attitude towards the sufferer. But a child cannot contribute much to the history of its malady. Its memory until one comes to its aid with analysis, does not reach far back. It is so taken up with the present that the past pales in comparison. Besides, it does not know itself when its abnormality began and when its nature first appeared to be different from that of other children. It has as yet little notion of comparing itself with others, and still less of self-appointed tasks by which it can measure its failures. Thus a children's analyst must in practice take the case history from the patient's parents. There is nothing else for it but to make all possible allowance for inaccuracies and misrepresentations arising from personal motives.

Contrariwise, we have in dream interpretation a field in which we can apply unchanged to children the methods of analysis of adults. During analysis the child dreams neither less nor more than the grown-up, the transparency or obscurity of the dream content conforms as in the case of adults to the strength of the resistance. Children's dreams are certainly easier to interpret, if indeed they are not always so simple as the examples given in *The Interpretation of Dreams*. We find in them every such distortion of wish-fulfilment as corresponds to the complicated neurotic organisation of the childish patient. But there is nothing easier to make the child grasp than dream interpretation. At the first account of a dream, I say "No dream can make itself out of nothing; it must have fetched every bit from somewhere"—and then I set off with the child in search of its origins. The child amuses itself with the pursuit of the individual dream elements as with a jigsaw puzzle, and follows up the separate images or words into real life situations with great satisfaction. Perhaps this comes about because the child still stands nearer to dreams than the adult; it may again be merely because it feels no surprise to find a meaning in dreams, not having heard the view that they have no meaning. In any case it is proud of a successful dream interpretation. And moreover I have often found that even unintelligent children, who in all other points were as inapt as possible for analysis, did not fail in dream-interpretation. I have conducted two such analyses for an extended period almost exclusively by using dreams.

But even where the associations to the child's dreams fail to appear, an interpretation is nevertheless often still possible. It is so much easier to know the child's situation, the daily happenings and significant people in its life. Often one may venture to insert the missing ideas into the interpretation from one's own knowledge of the situation. The two following examples of children's dreams, will merely serve to illustrate these circumstances.

In the fifth month of the analysis of a nine-year-old girl I eventually arrived at the discussion of her masturbation, which she could only admit even to herself with a strong feeling of guilt. She felt very hot sensations when masturbating, and her revulsion against her handling of her genitals extended to these feelings. She began to be afraid of fire and rebelled against wearing warm clothes. She could not see the flame burning in a gas water heater next her bedroom without fearing an explosion. One evening when the mother was away the nurse wanted to light the heater, but did not know how and called the elder brother to help. But he did not know how either. The little girl stood by and had the feeling that she ought to know how. The following night she dreamed of the same situation, but in the dream *she actually did help, but did it wrong and the heater exploded. As a punishment the nurse held her in the fire so that she would burn up.* She woke up in a great state of anxiety and awakened her mother at once to tell her the dream, adding (from her analytical knowledge) that it was certainly a punishment dream. She brought up no other ideas, but I could easily supply them in this case. Manipulating the heater stood for manipulating her own body, which she assumed her brother did too. "Doing it wrong" was the expression of her own condemnation, and the explosion probably represented her form of orgasm. The nurse, who was the natural person to admonish against masturbation, appropriately carried out the punishment.

Two months later she had another fire-dream with the following content: *"On the radiator there were two bricks of different colours. I knew that the house was going to catch fire and I was frightened. Then somebody came and took the bricks away."* When she woke up she had her hand on her genitals.

This time she associated an idea to a part of the dream, the bricks; she had been told that if you put bricks on your head you do not grow. From that the interpretation could be completed without difficulty. Stopping growing was one of the punishments for masturbation which she feared, and we recognised the significance of fire as a symbol of her sexual excitation from the earlier dream. Thus she masturbated in her sleep, was warned by the remembrance of all the prohibitions, and was frightened. The unknown person who took away the bricks was probably myself, with my soothing reassurances.

Not all dreams occurring in the analysis of children present so few difficulties in interpretation. But on the whole my little compulsion-neurotic was right when she would announce to me a dream of the preceding night as follows: "To-day I have a funny dream to tell you, but you and I will soon find out what it all means."

The interpretation of daydreams as well as of ordinary dreams plays an important part in the analysis of children. Several of the children with whom I gained my experience were great daydreamers, and the retailing of their fantasies became of the greatest assistance to me in analysis. It is usually very easy to induce children to recount their daydreams, once one has gained their confidence in other matters. They tell them more readily and are clearly less ashamed of them than adults, who condemn daydreaming as "childish." While the adult, from these considerations of shame and condemnation, usually only brings his daydreams into the analysis at a late stage and hesitatingly, in a child's analysis their appearance is often of great assistance in the difficult early stages. The following examples will give you three types of such fantasies.

The simplest type is the daydream as a reaction to an experience in the day. The little girl for example, whose dreams I have just mentioned, at the time when competition with her brothers and sisters was playing a part of great importance in her analysis, reacted to a supposed slight setback with the following daydream: *I wish I had never come into the world at all, I wish I could die. Sometimes I pretend I do die, and then come back into the world as an animal or a doll. But if I do come back into the world as a doll, I know who I mean to belong to—a little girl that my nurse was with before, who is specially nice and good. I want to be her doll and I would not mind at all being treated like they treat dolls. I would be a dear little baby and they could wash me and do anything to me. The little girl would like me best of all. Perhaps she would get another doll for Christmas but I would still be her favourite. She would never prefer any doll to the baby doll."* It is superfluous to add that of her brothers and sisters the two of whom she was particularly jealous were younger than she. Her current situation could not find clearer expression in any account or association than it did in this little fantasy.

The six-year-old compulsion-neurotic lived at the beginning of her analysis with friends of her family. She had one of her fits of naughtiness, which was much criticised by the other children. Her little girl friend even refused to sleep in the same room with her, which upset her very much. She told me in the analysis however that she had been good, that the nurse had given her a present of a little toy rabbit, and assured me at the same time that the other children liked sleeping with her very much. Then she recounted a daydream which she had suddenly had while she was resting. She had not felt at all that she was making it up. *"Once upon a time there was a little rabbit, whose family were not at all nice to him. They were going to send him to the slaughterhouse and have him slaughtered. But he found it out. He had a car which was very old but could still be driven. He went for it at night and got in and drove away. He came to a dear little house in which a little girl* (here she used her own name) *lived. She heard him crying downstairs and came down and let him in. Then he stayed to live with her."* Here the feeling of not being wanted, which she would willingly be spared both in my eyes and her own, shows itself quite transparently. She herself is twice present in the daydream—as the little unloved rabbit and as the little girl who treats him as well as she herself would like to be treated.

A more complicated second type is the continued day-dream.

With children who compose such "serial story" day-dreams it is often very easy to get on such terms that even in the earliest part of the analysis they will daily retail the new instalment. The current inward situation of the child can be reconstructed from these day-by-day continuations.

As an example of a third type I will mention a nine-year-old boy, whose daydreams, though certainly con-structed with varying people and circumstances, re-peated in innumerable situations the same outcome. He began his analysis with the narration of an abundance of such stored-up fantasies. In many of them the two principal personages were a hero and a king. The king threatened the hero, wanting to torture and slay him, and the hero escaped him in all possible ways. All tech-nical inventions, especially an air fleet, played a great part in the pursuit. A cutting-machine, which sent out sickle-like knives on each side when in motion, was also of great importance. The fantasy ended with the hero victorious, and doing everything to the king which the king wanted to do to him. Another of his daydreams depicted a teacher who punished and beat the children. The children eventually surrounded and overpowered her, and beat her to death. Still another had to do with a whipping-machine, in which in the end the torturer was locked instead of the captive for whom it was in-tended. He still possessed in his memory a whole col-lection of such fantasies with endless variations. With-out knowing anything more about the boy we can divine that all these fantasies are based on the defence against and revenge for a castration-threat; that is to say, the castration is to be carried out in the daydream on the very person who originally threatened it. You will agree that with such a beginning one can anticipate much of the later progress of the analysis.

A further technical auxiliary, which besides the use of dreams and daydreams comes very much to the fore in many of my analyses of children, is drawing; in three of my cases this for a time almost took the place of all other communications. Thus the little fire-dreamer, at the time when she was occupied with her castration complex, incessantly drew pictures of a fearful-looking monster in human shape, with protruding chin, long nose, an infinity of hair, and a frightful set of teeth. The name of this constantly recurring monster was "Bitey," and his function was clearly to bite off the male genital which he himself had developed in such manifold fashion on his own body. Another series of drawings which she made in great quantity during her visits, either as an accompaniment to her stories or in silence, portrayed all sorts of beings, children, birds, snakes and dolls, all with enormously extended arms and legs or beaks and tails. On another page in the same period she assembled all of a sudden all the things she wanted to be: a boy (so as to possess a male member), a doll (so as to be the best-beloved), a dog (which to her represented virility), and a sailor boy, whom she took from a fantasy in which she as a boy accompanied her father on a voyage round the world. Above all these figures was yet another drawing from a half-heard and half-invented fairy story—a witch pulling out a giant's hair; thus again a representation of castration for which at this time she blamed her mother. In strange contrast to this was a series of pictures from a much later period, in which a queen presented to a little princess standing before her a marvellous long-stemmed flower (obviously another penis-symbol).

The little compulsion-neurotic drew pictures of another kind. She occasionally accompanied her anal fantasies, which took up the first part of her analysis, with illustrations. For example, she portrayed an anal land of Cockayne, in which instead of the mounds of porridge and tarts of the fairy story the people had to eat their way through a monstrous accumulation of pats of excrement arranged in rows. Besides that however I possess a series of most delicately coloured pictures of flowers and gardens, which she painstakingly executed with much neatness and grace while retailing to me her very "dirty" anal daydreams.

But I fear that I have sketched for you, thus far, too ideal a picture of the conditions obtaining in the analysis of children. The family readily furnishes all requisite information; the child is disclosed as an eager dream-interpreter bringing a rich outpouring of daydreams and furnishing a series of interesting drawings, from all of which conclusions as to its unconscious impulses may be drawn. If all this is so, it is puzzling to see why the analysis of children has always been felt to be so difficult, or why so many analysts declare that they can make no headway in the treatment of children.

The solution is not far to seek. The child cancels all the foregoing advantages by reason of the fact that it refuses to associate. The analyst is thus plunged into perplexity, for the very method on which the analytical technique is founded becomes to all intents and purposes useless. It is obviously contrary to a child's nature to assume the easy recumbent position prescribed for the adult, to expunge by an effort of its own will all criticism of emerging ideas, to exclude nothing from its communications, and so to explore the surface of its consciousness.

It is indeed true that when one has attached a child to oneself in the ways I have described, and made oneself indispensable to it, one can make it do anything. Thus for once in a way it will occasionally associate on being invited to do so, for a short time and to please the analyst. Such an interpolation of associations may certainly be of the greatest use and bring sudden enlightenment in a difficult situation. But it will always be of the nature of temporary assistance and not the secure basis on which the whole analytical work can be founded.

I could sometimes ask one little girl, who in analysis proved particularly docile and amenable to my wishes and who with her great talent for drawing was especially visually perceptive, to "see pictures." She would then sit herself down in a remarkable crouching attitude and follow attentively her inward images. In this way she once actually gave me the solution to a long-drawn-out resistance situation. The preoccupation of that period was the struggle over masturbation and the detachment from her nurse, to whom she had retreated with redoubled affection so as to defend herself against my efforts at liberation. I asked her to see pictures and the first answer was "Nurse is flying away over the sea." This, with the addition of a vision of myself surrounded by a lot of dancing devils, meant that I would be sending the nurse away; and then she would have no defence against her masturbatory impulses and would be made "wicked" by me.

Here and there, and more frequently than these deliberate and invited associations, others, unintentional and ininvited, come to our help. I take the little compulsion-neurotic again as an example. At the climax of her analysis it was a matter of elucidating for her her hatred of her mother, against the knowledge of which she had previously defended herself by the creation of her "devil" as the impersonal deputy for all her hate-impulses. Although up to now she had co-operated readily, she began at this stage to shrink from further progress. At the same time however she relapsed at home into all manner of insolent naughtiness, from which I daily proved to her that one could only hate anyone to whom one behaved so badly. Finally she surrendered outwardly before these constantly recurring proofs, but demanded to know from me also the reason for such a hostile feeling towards her apparently well-loved mother. Here I declined to give further information, for I too was at the end of my knowledge. Thereupon after a moment's silence she said, "You know, I believe it is the fault of a dream I once had" (some weeks before) "that we never understood." I asked her to repeat it, which she did: *"All my dolls were there and my rabbit as well. Then I went away and the rabbit began to cry most dreadfully; and I was so sorry for it.* I believe I am always copying the rabbit now, and that is why I keep crying like it did." In reality of course it was the other way round—the rabbit copied her, not she the rabbit. In that dream she herself had taken the mother's place, and treated the rabbit as she had been treated by her. With this dream idea she had finally found the reproach which her consciousness always shrank from making towards her mother: that she had always gone away just when the child most needed her.

Some days later she repeated the process a second time. I pressed her, when her whole outlook had clouded over again after a temporary clearing, to contribute more on the same subject. She could not do so, but said suddenly in deep thought "It is so lovely at G.—, I should like so much to go there again." On closer question it became apparent that in a holiday in that place she must have passed one of her unhappiest times. Her elder brother had been sent back to his parents in the town because he had whooping cough, and she was isolated with the nurse and two younger children. She added spontaneously, "The nurse was always cross when I took the toys away from the little ones." Thus at that time the actual preference of the nurse for the younger children was added to the supposed preference of the parents for the brother. She felt herself neglected on all sides and re-acted in her own way. And now she had again found one of her deepest reproaches against her mother through a recollection, this time of the beauty of the countryside in that place.

I would not emphasise these three cases of surprising associations if such things occurred more frequently in the analysis of children. In analysing adults they are, of course, the rule.

This absence of the will to associate in children has led everyone who up to now has been concerned with the problem of children's analysis to seek for some sub-stitute or other. Dr. Hug-Hellmuth attempted to replace the knowledge obtained from an adult patient's free associations by playing with the child, seeing it in its own circle, and trying to become familiar with all its intimate daily circumstances. Mrs. Melanie Klein sub-stitutes for the adult association technique the play tech-nique with children described in her publications. She starts from the premise that action is more natural for a little child than speech, and puts at its disposal a host of tiny playthings, a world in miniature, so that it can act in the playworld. She puts all the actions which the child carries out in this way on a par with the adult's spoken ideas, and attends them with interpretations as we are used to do with adult patients. It looks at first sight as though a distressing gap in the technique of children's analysis had been filled up in an unobjection-able way. I wish to reserve however for my next lecture an examination of the theoretical foundation of this play-technique, and to set it in relation to the last aspect of our present subject, the rôle of transference in chil-dren's analysis.

THIRD LECTURE

The Rôle of Transference in the Analysis of Children

Ladies and Gentlemen. I will go briefly over the ground covered at our last meeting.

We directed attention to the methods of the analysis of children; we remarked that we have to put the case-history together from information furnished by the family, instead of relying exclusively upon that given by the patient; we became familiar with the child as a good dream-interpreter, and evaluated the significance of daydreams and imaginative drawings as technical auxiliaries. On the other hand I had to report that children are not inclined to enter into free association, and by this refusal oblige us to look for some substitute for this most essential of aids in the analysis of adults. We concluded with a description of one of these substitute methods, postponing its theoretical evaluation until to-day.

The play technique worked out by Mrs. Melanie Klein is certainly valuable for observing the child. Instead of taking the time and trouble to pursue it into its domestic environment we establish at one stroke the whole of its known world in the analyst's room, and let it move about in it under the analyst's eye but at first without his interference. In this way we have the opportunity of getting to know the child's various reactions, the strength of its aggressive impulses or of its sympathies, as well as its attitude to the various things and persons represented by the toys. There is this advantage over the observation of real conditions, that the toy environment is manageable and amenable to the child's will, so that it can carry out in it all the actions which in the real world, so much bigger and stronger than itself, remain confined to a fantasy-existence. All these merits make the use of the Klein play-method almost indispensable for familiarisation with small children, who are not yet capable of verbal self-expression.

Mrs. Klein however takes an important further step in the employment of this technique. She assumes the same status for these play-actions of the child as for the free associations of the adult patient, and translates as she goes along the actions undertaken by the child in this way into corresponding thoughts; that is to say, she tries to find beneath everything done in play its underlying symbolic function. If the child overturns a lamp-post or a toy figure she interprets it as something of an aggressive impulse against the father; a deliberate collision between two cars as evidence of an observation of sexual union between the parents. Her procedure consists in accompanying the child's activities with translations and interpretations, which themselves—like the interpretation of the adult's free associations—exert a further influence upon the patient.

Let us examine the justification for equating the child's play activity with the adult's free association. The adult's ideas are "free," that is to say the patient has divested his thoughts of all direction and influence, but his attitude is nevertheless influenced by a certain consideration—that he who is associating has set himself to be analysed. The child lacks this attitude. I think it is possible, as I have explained before, to give the children some idea of the purpose of analysis. But the children for whom Mrs. Klein has worked out her play-technique, in the first infantile period, are too young to be influenced in this way. Mrs. Klein considers it as one of the important advantages of her method that by it she is

saved the necessity of such a preparation of the child.
But if the child's play is not dominated by the same
purposive attitude as the adult's free association, there
is no justification for treating it as having the same
significance. Instead of being invested with symbolic
meaning it may sometimes admit of a harmless explanation. The child who upsets a toy lamp-post may on its
walk the day before have come across some incident in
connection with such an object; the car collision may
be reproducing some happening in the street; and the
child who runs towards a lady visitor and opens her
handbag is not necessarily, as Mrs. Klein maintains,
thereby symbolically expressing its curiosity as to
whether its mother's womb conceals another little
brother or sister, but may be connecting some experience of the previous day when someone brought it a
little present in a similar receptacle. Indeed with an
adult we do not consider ourselves justified in ascribing
a symbolic significance to every one of his acts or ideas,
but only to those which arise under the influence of
the analytical situation which he has accepted.

In reply to this objection to the Klein technique it
may be said that a child's play is certainly open to the
harmless interpretation just suggested, but why does it
reproduce just those particular scenes with the lamp-
post or the cars? Is it not just the symbolic significance
behind these observations which cause them to be pre-
ferred and reproduced before any others in the analytical hour? It is true, the argument may proceed, that the
child lacks in its actions the purposive attitude of the
analytical situation, which guides the adult. But perhaps
it does not need it at all. The adult must renounce the
guidance of his thoughts by a conscious effort of will and
leave their direction entirely to his unconscious impulses. But the child may require no such deliberate

modification of its situation. Perhaps it is at all times and in every piece of play entirely surrendered to the domination of its unconscious.

It is not easy to determine by an exchange of theoretical arguments the question of whether the equation of children's play with adults' free association is justifiable or not. This is obviously a matter for review in the light of practical experience.

Let us try criticism on another point. We know that Mrs. Klein utilises for interpretation, besides the things which the child does with the toys provided, all its procedure towards the objects found in her room or towards her own person. Here again she follows strictly the example of adult analysis. We certainly feel justified in drawing into the analysis all the patient's behaviour towards us during the visit, and all the little voluntary and involuntary actions which we observe him to perform. In this we are relying upon the state of transference in which he finds himself, which can invest even otherwise trivial behaviour with symbolic significance.

Here the question arises as to whether a child finds itself in the same transference situation as the adult; in what manner and in what forms its transference-impulses come to expression; and in what they lend themselves to interpretation. We have come to the important consideration, of *the rôle of transference as a technical expedient in the analysis of children*. The decision on this question will at the same time furnish fresh material to controvert or support Mrs. Klein's contention.

I explained in the first lecture how I took great pains to establish in the child a strong attachment to myself, and to bring it into a relationship of real dependence on me. I would not have tried so hard to do this, if I had thought the analysis of children could be carried out without a transference of this kind. But the affectionate attachment, the positive transference as it is called in analytical terminology, is the prerequisite for all later work. The child in fact will only believe the loved person, and it will only accomplish something to please that person.

The analysis of children requires much more from this attachment than in the case of adults. There is an educational as well as an analytical purpose with which we shall later be concerned in more detail: Successful upbringing always not only in children's analysis—stands or falls with the pupil's attachment to the person in charge of it. And we cannot say in regard to the analysis of children that the establishment of a transference is in itself enough for our purpose, regardless of whether it is friendly or hostile. We know that with an adult we can get through long periods with a negative transference, which we turn to our account through consistent interpretation and reference to its origins. But with a child negative impulses towards the analyst—however revealing they may be in many respects—are essentially inconvenient, and should be dealt with as soon as possible. The really fruitful work always takes place with a positive attachment.

I have described the establishment of this affectionate tie during our discussion of the introductory phase to the analysis of children. Its expression in fantasies and small or larger actions is hardly distinguishable from the equivalent processes in adult patients. We are made to feel the negative reactions at every point where we attempt to assist a fragment of repressed material towards liberation from the unconscious, thereby drawing upon ourselves the resistance of the ego. At such a time we appear to the child as the dangerous and to-be-feared tempter, and we bring on ourselves all the expressions of hatred and repulsion with which at other times it treats its own forbidden instinctual impulses.

I will give an account of a positive transference-fantasy from the six-year-old obsessional patient. The external occasion for it was furnished by myself, for I had visited her in her own home and stayed for her evening bath. She opened her visit on the next day with the words, "you visited me in my bath and next time I'll come and visit you in yours." Some while later she retailed for me the daydream which she had composed in bed before going to sleep, after I had gone away. I add her own explanatory asides in brackets.

"All the rich people did not like you. And your father who was very rich did not like you at all. (That means I am angry with your father, don't you think?) And you liked no one and gave lessons to no one. And my father and mother hated me and so did John and Billy and Mary and all the people in the world hated us, even the people we did not know, even the dead people. So you liked only me and I liked only you and we always stayed together. All the others were very rich but we two were quite poor. We had nothing, not even clothes for they took away everything we had. There was only the sofa left in the room and we slept on that together. But we were quite happy together. And then we thought we ought to have a baby. So we mixed a-a and cissies to make a baby. But then we thought that was not a nice thing to make a baby out of. So we began to mix flower-petals and things that gave me a baby. For the baby was in me. It stayed in me quite a long while (my mother told me that, that babies stay quite a long while in their mothers) and then the doctor took it out. But I was not a bit sick (mothers usually are, my mother said). The baby was very sweet and cunning and so we thought we'd like to be just as cunning and changed ourselves to be very small. I was 'so' high and you were 'so' high. (That is, I think because in our lesson last week we found out that I wanted to be like Billy and Mary.) And as we had nothing at all we started to make ourselves a house out of rose-leaves, and beds out of rose-leaves and pillows and mattresses all out of rose-leaves sewn together. Where the little holes were left we put something white in. Instead of wall-paper we had the thinnest glass and the walls were carved in different patterns. The chairs were made of glass too but we were so light that we were not too heavy for them. (I think I left my mother out because I was angry with her for not coming to see me.)" Then there followed a detailed description of the furniture and all the things that were made for the house. The daydream was obviously spun out in this direction until she went to sleep, laying special emphasis on the point that our initial poverty was finally quite made up for and that in the end we had much nicer things than all the first mentioned rich people.

The same little patient at other times related how she was warned against me from within. The inner voice said, "Don't believe Anna Freud. She tells lies. She will not help you and will only make you worse. She will change your face too, so that you look uglier. Everything she says is not true. Just be tired, stay quietly in bed and don't go to her to-day." But she always told this voice to be silent and said to it that it should be told of first of all in the next appointment.

Another small patient envisaged me, at the time when we were discussing her masturbation, in all sorts of degrading rôles—as a beggar, as a poor old woman, and once as just myself but standing in the middle of my room with devils dancing round me.

You will notice that we become the object towards which the patient's friendly or hostile impulses are directed, just as we do in the case of adults. It might seem from these examples that a child makes a good transference. Unfortunately that is not really true. The child indeed enters into the liveliest relations with the analyst, and evinces a multitude of reactions which it has acquired in the relationship with its parents; it gives us most important hints on the formation of its character in the fluctuation, intensity, and expression of its feelings; but it forms no transference-neurosis.

The analysts amongst you will know what I mean by this. The adult neurotic gradually transforms, in the course of analytic treatment, the symptom on account of which he sought this remedy. He gives up the old objects on which his fantasies were hitherto fixed, and centres his neurosis anew upon the person of the analyst. As we put it, he substitutes transference symptoms for his previous symptoms, transposes his existing neurosis, of whatever kind, into a transference-neurosis, and displays all his abnormal reactions in relation to the new transference person, the analyst. On this new ground, where the analyst feels at home, he can follow up with the patient the origin and growth of the individual symptoms; and on this cleared field of operations there then takes place the final struggle, for gradual insight into the malady and the discovery to the patient of the unconscious processes within him.

There are two possible reasons why this cannot be brought about in the case of a small child. One lies within the psychological structure of the child itself, the other in the child's analyst.

The child is not, like the adult, ready to produce a new edition of its love-relationships, because, as one might say, the old edition is not yet exhausted. Its original objects, the parents, are still real and present as love-objects—not only in fantasy as with the adult neurotic; between them and the child exist all the relations of everyday life, and all its gratifications and disappointments still in reality depend on them. The analyst enters this situation as a new person, and will probably share with the parents the child's love or hate. But there is no necessity for the child to exchange the parents for him, since compared to them he has not the advantages which the adult finds when he can exchange his fantasy-objects for a real person. Let us in this connection reconsider Mrs. Klein's method. She maintains that when a child evinces hostility towards her in the first visit, repulsing or even beginning to strike her, one may see in that a proof of the child's ambivalent attitude towards its mother. The hostile components of this ambivalence are merely displaced onto the analyst. But I believe the truth of the matter is different. The more tenderly a little child is attached to its own mother, the fewer friendly impulses it has towards strangers. We see this most clearly with the baby, who shows only anxious rejection towards everyone other than its mother or nurse. Indeed the converse obtains. It is especially with children who are accustomed to little loving treatment at home, and are not used to showing or receiving any strong affection, that a positive relationship is often most quickly established. They obtain from the analyst what they have up till now expected in vain from the original love objects.

On the other hand, the behaviour of the children's analyst, as we have described him, is not such as to produce a transference that can be well interpreted. We know how we bear ourselves in the analysis of adults for this purpose. We remain impersonal and shadowy, a blank page on which the patient can inscribe his transference-fantasies, somewhat after the way in which at the cinema a picture is thrown upon an empty screen. We avoid either issuing prohibitions, or allowing gratifications. If in spite of this we seem to the patient forbidding or encouraging, it is easy to make it clear to him that he has brought the material for this impression from his own past.

But the children's analyst must be anything but a shadow. We have already remarked that he is a person of interest to the child, endowed with all sorts of interesting and attractive qualities. The educational implications which, as you will hear, are involved in the analysis, result in the child knowing very well just what seems to the analyst desirable or undesirable, and what he sanctions or disapproves of. And such a well-defined and in many respects novel personality is unfortunately a bad transference-object, of little use when it comes to interpreting the transference. The difficulty here is, as though, to use our former illustration, the screen on which a film was to be projected already bore another picture. The more elaborate and brightly-coloured it is, the more will it tend to efface the outlines of what is superimposed.

For these reasons the child forms no transference-neurosis. In spite of all its positive and negative impulses towards the analyst it continues to display its abnormal reactions where they were displayed before—in the home circle. Because of this the children's analyst is obliged to take into account not only what happens under his own eye but also what occurs in the real scene of the neurotic reactions, i.e. the child's home. Here we come to an infinity of practical technical difficulties in the analysis of children, which I only lay broadly before you without going into actual detail. Working from this standpoint we are dependent upon a permanent news-service about the child; we must know the people in its environment and be sure to some extent of what their reactions to the child are. In the ideal case, we share our work with the persons who are actually bringing up the child; just as we share with them the child's affection or hostility.

Where the external conditions, or the personalities of the parents, do not allow of such co-operative treatment, certain material for the analysis eludes us. On this account I had to conduct some analyses of children almost exclusively by means of dreams and daydreams. There was nothing interpretable in the transference and much of the day-to-day symptomatic neurotic material never became available to me.

But there are ways and means to bring about an equation of the child's situation to that of the adult (so much better suited for the carrying through of analysis); and so to force the child into a transference-neurosis. This may become necessary where it is a case of severe neurotic illness in an environment hostile either to analysis or the child. In such a case the child would have to be removed from its family and placed in some suitable institution. As there is no such institution in existence at present we are at full liberty to imagine one, say a home supervised by the children's analyst himself, or—less far-fetched—a school where psychoanalytical principles predominate and the work is attuned to co-operation with the analyst. In both cases a symptom-free period would first occur, in which the child accustoms itself to the new and favourable surroundings. The better it feels at this time, the more unapt and unwilling for analysis shall we find it. We shall probably do best to leave it quite undisturbed. Only when it has "acclimatised itself," that is to say when under the influence of the realities of everyday life it has formed an attachment to the new environment, beside which the original objects gradually pale; when it allows its symptoms to revive again in this new existence, and groups its abnormal reactions around new personages; when it has thus formed its transference-neurosis—will it become analysable once more.

In an institution of the first sort, managed by the children's analyst (and at present we cannot even judge whether such an arrangement is to be desired) it would then be a matter of an actual transference-neurosis in the sense of the adult's with the analyst as focal object. In the other sort we should simply have artificially bettered the home environment, creating a substitute home which so to say allows us to see into it, as seems necessary for the analytical work, and the reactions of which towards the child we can control and regulate.

Thus the removal of the child from its home might appear to be the most practical solution. But when we come to consider the termination of a child's analysis, we shall see how many objections there are to it. By this expedient we forestall the natural development at a crucial stage, forcing the child's premature detachment from the parental objects at a time when it neither is capable of any independence in its emotional life, nor has at its disposal, owing to external circumstances, any freedom in the choice of new love-objects. Even if we insist on a very long duration for the analysis of children there still remains in most cases a hiatus between its termination and the development of puberty, during which the child needs education, protection, and guidance in every sense of the words. But what gives us any assurance that after we have secured a successful resolution of the transference the child will find of itself the way to the right objects? It returns home at a time when it has become a stranger there, and its further guidance is now perhaps entrusted to the very persons from whom we have forcibly detached it. On inner grounds it is not capable of self-reliance. We are thus placing it in a position of renewed difficulty, in which it will find again most of the original elements of its conflict. It can now take either once more the path to neurosis or, if this is closed to it by the successful outcome of the analytical treatment, the opposite line of open rebellion. From the purely therapeutical point of view this may seem an advantage; but from that of social adjustment which in the child's case matters most in the end, it is certainly none.

FOURTH LECTURE

The Analysis of Children and Their Upbringing

Ladies and Gentlemen. We have, so far, considered two aspects of the analysis of children and to-day I will turn to the third and perhaps most important.

Let me once more retrace our progress. The first part was concerned, as you may remember, with the introductory phase in the analysis of children. This has no bearing on analytical theory. I did not describe all those paltry and childish methods and occupations, crochetting, knitting, and games, all the various means of enticement, because I consider them important for analysis, but on the contrary rather to show what an intractable subject the child is, and how it is not amenable to the best-tried methods of scientific therapy but absolutely requires that its own childish peculiarities should be appropriately matched. Whatever we embark on with a child, whether to teach it arithmetic or geography, whether intending to educate or analyse, we must always first establish a very definite emotional relationship with it. The harder the work to be done, the higher must be the strain-capacity of this attachment. The introduction to the treatment, that is to say the establishment of this tie, thus follows its own rules, determined by childish nature and temporarily independent of analytical theory and technique.

The second part of my exposition dealt with analysis proper, and surveyed the paths whereby one can approach a child's unconscious. It is disappointing that the very best and most specific expedients in the analysis of adults are not available for that of children, and that we must fall short of many of the obligations imposed by scientific theory and obtain our material where we can find it—much as we do in the ordinary way if we wish to enter into someone's private life. I suspect there is a further disappointment. Since I have been doing analysis of children I have often been asked by analytical colleagues, whether I have not gained some closer understanding than can be had from the analysis of adults of the developmental processes of the first two years of life, towards which our analytical investigations are ever more urgently directed. The child, they say, is still so much nearer to this significant period, its repressions must be still so much less deeply embedded, the overlaid material so much easier of access, that there should surely be special facilities for investigation.

So far I have always had to answer these questions with a negative. The material which the child affords us is indeed, as you may have noticed from my illustrations, especially clear and unequivocal. It supplies all sorts of evidence as to the contents of children's neuroses, the presentation of which I shall reserve for another occasion. It brings much welcome confirmation of facts which up to now we have only been able to assert on conclusions drawn from the analysis of adults. But so far as my experience goes, with the technique I have described, it does not take us beyond the boundaries where the child's speech-faculty begins—and so where it thinks in the same way as we do. The theoretical explanation of this is easy to find. What we learn in the analysis of adults about this "prehistoric" period is brought to light through free associations and the interpretation of the transference-reactions; the very two auxiliaries which leave us in the lurch in the analysis of children. Besides, our situation may be compared to that of an ethnologist, who would also seek in vain for a short cut to prehistory in studying a primitive people instead of a cultured race. He would miss in the primitive people all the help from the creation of myth and saga which enables him to draw conclusions in the case of the cultured people. Similarly with the small child we lack the reaction-formations and cover-memories which are only constructed in the course of the latency period, and from which the later analysis can extract the material condensed in them. Here again, therefore, the analysis of children offers no advantage over that of adults but is in fact less able to extract unconscious material.

And now for the third aspect, the utilisation of the analytical material which with such painful preparation and by so many paths and bypaths we have brought to light. You will be prepared by now to hear a good deal that is unexpected and deviates from the classical rules.

Let us first reconsider in rather more detail the corresponding situation in the adult patient. His neurosis is, as we know, entirely an internal affair. It is played out between three factors, his instinctual unconscious, his Ego, and his Super-ego, which last represents the ethical and æsthetic demands of society. The task of analysis is to raise the conflict between these protagonists to a higher level, by making conscious what is unconscious. The instinctual impulses were up till now removed from the influence of the Super-ego by the condition of repression. Analysis frees them and makes them accessible to the influence of the Super-ego by which their further fate will then be determined. Conscious criticism, the rejection of part, takes the place of repression, while of the remainder part can be sublimated away from its sexual aims and part may be allowed gratification. This favourable outcome is to be ascribed to the fact that the patient's Ego, between the time when it instituted its original repressions and the point when analysis achieves its task of liberation, has undergone its whole ethical and intellectual development, and so is in a position to make other decisions than those which were originally open to it. The instinctual life must submit to various restrictions, and the Super-ego must surrender many of its exaggerated pretensions. On the common ground of activity in consciousness a synthesis between the two is brought about.

And now compare with this the conditions of the child patient's case. The child's neurosis is also certainly an internal affair, determined by the same three forces, the instinctual life, the Ego and the Super-ego. But we are already prepared to find that at two points in the child's case the outer world penetrates deeply into its inner situation as a factor indeed inconvenient for the analysis but organically important. In discussing the introductory phase required for the analysis of children we were obliged to ascribe so important a factor as insight into the malady, not to the child itself, but to the people surrounding it; and in describing the transference-situation we demonstrated that the analyst is obliged to share the child's available hostile and loving impulses with the original objects of these feelings. We are thus not surprised that the outer world affects the mechanism of infantile neurosis and analysis more deeply than in the adult case.

We have said that the Super-ego of an adult individual has become the representative of moral demands made by the society in which he lives. We know that it owes its origin to the identification with the first and most important of the child's love objects, the parents; to them society had transferred the task of establishing its current ethical claims on the child and enforcing the restrictions upon instinct which it prescribes. Thus what was originally a personal obligation felt towards the parents, only turns into an Ego-ideal, independent of its prototypes, in the course of development from object-love for the parents to identification with them.

In the child's case however there is as yet no question of such independence. Detachment from the first loved objects lies still in the future, and identification, while the original object-love is maintained, will only be accomplished gradually and piecemeal. A Super-ego indeed exists, and many of the interactions between it and the Ego seem even at this early period analogous to those of the later and mature development. But the "constant relation" between this Super-ego and the objects to which it owes its establishment must not be overlooked; we might compare it to that between two receptacles connected together. If in the outer world the level of good relations with the parents rises, so does the prestige of the Super-ego and the energy with which it enforces its claims. If the former is lowered, the Super-ego is diminished as well.

Let us take the infant as the first example. When the mother or nurse has succeeded in accustoming the little child to the control of its excretory functions, we soon get the impression that it fulfils these requirements of cleanliness not only for the sake of the adult (for love or fear of her), but that it has itself some interest in the matter, is pleased with its own cleanliness or vexed if it has an "accident." We notice over and over again, however, that a subsequent separation from the person who has inculcated this cleanliness, such as a temporary removal from the mother or a change of nurse, puts the new achievement into jeopardy. The child will become just as dirty as it was before it learnt the new ways and will only re-acquire them when the mother returns or an attachment is formed to the new nurse. Nevertheless the impression that the child had itself felt an obligation to cleanliness was not altogether deceptive.

The inner prompting exists, but is only worth while to the child while the person responsible for its establishment retains her place as loved object in the outer world. Where the object-relationship lapses, so does the satisfaction in fulfilling the obligation.

But even at the opening of the latency-period the same factors apply. From the analysis of adults we can find ample confirmation of how much any dislocation of a child's ties with its parents may disturb its moral development and formation of character. If at this time it loses its parents through separation of any kind, or if as objects they are depreciated in its eyes, perhaps through some such cause as a mental illness or criminality, its already extensively-constructed Super-ego is in danger of being lost or depreciated too; so that it can reoppose no real inner volition to the instinctual impulses which press for satisfaction. The origin of many anti-social and character abnormalities may be explained in this way.

To illustrate these conditions, even at the end of the latency-period, I will add an example from the analysis of a pre-adolescent boy. I once asked him, whether he was ever aware of any thoughts which one would prefer not to have. He answered "Yes, when one wants to steal something." I asked him to describe such an occasion, and he said "For example when I am alone at home and there is some fruit, and my father and mother have gone out without giving me any. Then I get to thinking how I should like to take some. But then I think about something else because I don't mean to steal." I asked if he was always stronger than these thoughts. He said yes, he had never stolen anything. "What do you do," I said, "when they are very strong?" "I still don't take anything," he said triumphantly, "for then I am afraid of my father."

You observe that his Super-ego has reached a considerable degree of independence, which was expressed in his own wish not to be a thief. But when the temptation was too strong he must bring in the support of the person to whom this wish owed its existence, namely the father with the warnings and threats of punishment associated with him. Another child in his place would perhaps have called to mind his love for his mother.

From this weakness and dependence of the claims of the child's Ego-ideal follows another observation, which can be confirmed any number of times: the child has a double set of morals, one for the grown-up world and one for itself and its contemporaries. We know for example that at a certain age a child begins to feel shame, that is to say it avoids showing itself naked, or performing its excretory functions before strange grown-ups and later even before those best known to it. But we know too that the same child will undress without any shame before other children, and they will often want to go to the lavatory together. Again, we can establish the surprising fact that a child will only be disgusted at certain things in the presence of grown-ups, and thus as it were under pressure from them, while when it is alone or with other children no such reaction appears. I remember a ten-year-old boy who on a walk suddenly pointed to a cow-pat and exclaimed with interest "Look, how funny that is!" The next moment he realised his mistake and blushed. Later he excused himself to me, saying he had not at first seen what it was or he would never have mentioned it. But I know from the same boy that when he is with his friends he talks about the excretory functions with amusement and no embarrassment. He also once assured me that when he is alone he can touch his own excrement with his hand without any particular feeling, but when any grown-up is there he finds it very difficult even to mention it.

Shame and disgust are important reaction-formations

designed to restrain the child's anal and exhibitionistic impulses from breaking through to gratification; but even when they are fully established, they depend upon the relationship with the adult object for their maintenance and efficacy.

With these observations as to the dependent stage of the childish Super-ego, and the child's double morals in relation to shame and disgust, we have arrived at the most important difference between the analysis of children and of adults. The former is by no means an entirely private affair, played out exclusively between two persons, the analyst and his patient. Insofar as the childish Super-ego has not yet become the impersonal representative of the obligations undertaken at the behest of the outer world, insofar as it is still organically connected with it, the relevant outer world objects play an important rôle in the analysis itself, and especially in its last part, the utilisation of the instinctual impulses which have been freed from repression.

Let us resume once more the comparison with the adult neurotic. We said that in his analysis we only had to reckon with his instinctual life, his Ego and his Super-ego; we need not trouble ourselves with the fate of the impulses which have emerged from the unconscious. These come under the influence of his Super-ego, which bears the responsibility for their further employment.

Where is this responsibility to lie in the case of a child's analysis? Is it to rest with those concerned with the child's upbringing, with whom its Super-ego is still inseparably bound up, that is, with its parents?

But awkward considerations are involved here. It was these same parents or guardians whose exorbitant requirements drove the child into an excess of repression and into neurosis. They, with their unchanged outlook are the very people who are now called upon to help in its recovery. Only in the most favourable cases have they learnt enough from the child's illness to be ready to mitigate their demands. Thus it seems dangerous to turn responsibility for the newly-liberated instinctual life over to them. There is too great risk that the child will be forced once more into the path to repression and neurosis. In such circumstances it would have been more economical to have omitted altogether the wearisome and painful process of liberation by analysis.

Again, in the child's case there is no such long interval betwen the formation of the neurosis and its resolution through analysis as there is in the case of the adult patient, who between these two stages undergoes his whole Ego-development, so that the being who made the original choice can hardly be called the same person as he who undertakes its revision. Would it be admissible to declare the child, just because of its neurosis and its analysis, prematurely of age; and expect from it itself the important decisions as to how it shall henceforward deal with the impulses now placed at its disposal? I do not know to what ethical basis it could have resort, to what criteria or practical considerations, to enable it to find a way through these difficulties. I think that, left alone and with every outer support withdrawn, it can only find one single short and convenient path—that of direct gratification. We know however from analytical theory and practice that, in the very interest of preventing neurosis, it is desirable to avoid too much direct gratification at any stage of a child's necessarily perverse sexuality. Otherwise fixation on the once-experienced pleasure will prove to be a hindrance to further normal development, and the urge for its revival a dangerous incentive to regression from later stages.

So it seems to me that there remains but one solution for this difficult situation. The analyst must claim for himself liberty to guide the child at this important point, so as to be able to make secure, to some extent, the achievement of the analysis. Under his influence the child must learn how to conduct itself in regard to its instinctual life, and his views must in the end determine what part of the infantile sexual impulses must be suppressed or rejected as unemployable in the cultural world; how much or how little can be allowed direct gratification; and what must be guided into the path of sublimation, for which process all the available resources of education can then be used. We may say in short, that *the analyst must succeed in putting himself in the place of the child's Ego-ideal for the duration of the analysis;* he ought not to begin his analytical work of liberation until he has made sure that the child is eager to follow his lead. The position of authority about which we spoke at the beginning, in connection with the introductory phase in the analysis of children, at this stage becomes essential; before the child can give the highest place in its emotional life, that of the Ego-ideal, to this new love object which ranks with the parents, it must feel that the analyst's authority is even greater than theirs.

If the child's parents have learnt something from its illness, and show an inclination to conform to the analyst's requirements, a real division of analytic and educational labour between home and analyst becomes possible—or rather a co-operation between the two. The child's education suffers no interruption even at the termination of the analysis, but passes back, wholly and directly, from the hands of the analyst into those of the now more understanding parents.

But if the parents use their influence to work against the analyst the result, since the child is emotionally attached to both, is a situation similar to that in an unhappy marriage where the child has become an object of contention. When the scene is set thus we cannot be

surprised if all the injurious consequences for the formation of character, with which we are familiar in such
cases, occur here as well. In the one instance the child
plays father and mother, in the other analyst and home,
against each other, and in both he uses the conflict as a
means of escape from all obligations. There is peril in
these conditions if a child in a resistance-situation is enabled so to prevail with the parents against the analyst
that they break off the analysis. The child is lost to the
analyst at the very worst moment, in a state of resistance
and negative transference, and is sure to take advantage
in the most undesirable ways of all the liberations already secured by the analysis. To-day I would not undertake the analysis of a child where the personalities of the
parents, or their analytical understanding, did not provide a guarantee against such an outcome.

I will give one last example to illustrate how necessary
it is that the analyst should be in control of the relationship between the child's Ego and its instincts.

When I had brought the six-year-old compulsion-neurotic to the point of allowing her "devil" to speak, she
began to communicate to me a large number of anal
fantasies, hesitatingly at first but soon with ever increas-
ing boldness and detail as she saw that no expressions of
displeasure on my part were forthcoming. Gradually the
analytical hour became entirely given up to anal con-
fidences, and was the repository of all the daydreams of
this kind which otherwise oppressed her. While she
talked in this way with me the constant oppression was
relieved. She herself called the time with me her "rest-
hour." She once said "My time with you, Anna Freud,
is my rest-hour. I don't have to restrain my devil. But
no," she went on, "I have another rest, when I am
asleep." Thus during analysis and sleep she was clearly
relieved from the equivalent of the adult's constant ex-

penditure of energy in maintaining repression. Her relief showed itself above all in an altered nature, lively and alert.

After a time she went a step further. She began to show something of her hitherto strictly guarded fantasies and anal ideas at home as well, making for example, when a dish came onto the table, a half-audible comparison or a "smutty" joke to the other children. The lady who then had the care of the child came to me for advice as to what to do. At that time I was still inexperienced, and I took the situation lightly, advising that one should neither acquiesce in nor dissent from such small manifestations, but simply let them pass unnoticed. The effect was unexpected. The child lost all moderation, carried over into her home all the ideas to which she had previously only given expression during analysis, and completely revelled, as she had with me, in her anal notions, comparisons, and expressions. The grown-ups in the house soon found this intolerable, and lost all appetite—especially on account of the child's behaviour at the common dinner table; and soon it happened that one after another, children as well as grown-ups, left the room in silent disapproval. My little patient had behaved like a pervert or a mentally afflicted adult, and thereby put herself beyond the pale of society. Since she was not penalised by being removed from the company of the others, the consequence was that they avoided her. By now she had abandoned all restraints in other respects as well. In a few days she had become transformed into a cheerful, over-bold and naughty child, by no means dissatisfied with herself.

Then came the guardian to me a second time, to complain. She said the state of affairs was unendurable. What ought she to do? Could she tell the child that talking of such things was not in itself wicked, but ask her to give it up at home for her sake? I did not agree to this suggestion. I had to realise that I had made a blunder, in crediting the child's Super-ego with an independent inhibitory strength which it did not possess. As soon as the important people in the outer world had relaxed their requirements the child's Ego-ideal, which was previously so strict and had been strong enough to bring forth a whole series of obsessional symptoms, suddenly became compliant. I had relied on this compulsive strictness and had been incautious; thereby I had not even forwarded the analysis. I had for a while made out of an inhibited, obsessional child a naughty, one might say perverted, one. But I had ruined the situation for my work. This emancipated child now had her "rest-hour" all day long, and considerably abated her enthusiasm for working with me; she no longer furnished proper material for it, for this was spread over the whole day instead of being reserved for the analysis, and she had temporarily lost the insight into the malady which is so necessary. The maxim that gratification should be withheld, if analysis is to be successful has even greater application to the analysis of children than to that of adults.

Fortunately the situation was not so bad as it looked and in practice it was easy to solve it. I bade the guardian do nothing further, and have a little patience. I would bring the child to order again, only I could not promise how soon the result would show. On the child's next visit I acted energetically; I said all this was a breach of our agreement; I had thought she was going to tell me all those things, so as to be rid of them, but now I saw that this was by no means so. She meant to tell them to everybody, for the pleasure of doing so. I had nothing against that, but in that case I could not see that she had any further use for me; we could simply give up our hours together and leave her pleasure to her. But if she remained of her first intention, she must tell these things only to me and to no one else. The more she refrained from at home, the more would occur to her with me; the more I would know about her and the more I would be able to rid her of. She must now choose between the alternatives.

She went very pale and reflected for some time, and then looked at me and said, with the same thoughtful comprehension as on the first occasion "If you say that that is how it is I will not talk like that any more." With that her obsessional conscientiousness returned. From that day no mention of the objectionable subjects crossed her lips again at home. She was re-transformed, but she had again become, from a naughty and perverted child, an inhibited and apathetic one.

I had to accomplish a similar transformation of the same patient several more times in the course of her treatment. Always when she escaped, on analytical liberation from her unusually severe compulsion-neurosis, to the other extreme, to naughtiness and perversion, there remained nothing for it but for me to bring about the neurosis again and restore the already vanished "devil" once more to his place; each time naturally in diminishing degrees and with greater precautions and gentleness than home education had used, until finally I got the child to hold a middle course between the two extremes.

I would not have enlarged upon this example if it were not that it serves to illustrate all the characteristics of the analysis of children put forward in this last section of our discussion: the fact that a child's Super-ego is weak; that Super-ego demands and neurosis are dependent on the outer world; that the child is unable to control the emancipated instincts; and that the analyst himself must guide them.[1] The analyst accordingly combines in his own person two difficult and diametrically opposed functions: he has to analyse and educate, that is to say in the same breath he must allow and forbid, loosen and bind again. If he does not succeed in this, analysis becomes the child's charter for all the ill conduct prohibited by society. But if he succeeds, he undoes a piece of wrong education and abnormal development, and so procures for the child, or whoever controls its destiny, an opportunity to improve matters.

In the case of an adult's analysis, we do not compel the patient to be well at the end of it. What he shall do with the choice newly offered to him lies with him; whether he will once more take the path into neurosis, whether his Ego-development permits his taking the opposite way to extensive instinctual gratification, or whether he will achieve the mean between the two, a real synthesis of the two forces within him. We cannot force the parents of our small patients, either, to take a reasonable course with the child when it is returned to them. The analysis of children is no insurance against all the mis-chances which the child's future may hold. It works above all on the past; thereby indeed it provides a cleared and improved ground for future development.

From the conditions which I have described you will have gleaned an important clue as to the indications for the analysis of children. These indications are not comprised solely in the fact of the child having a certain malady. The analysis of children belongs essentially in the analytical milieu, and must for the present be confined to the children of analysts or of people who have been analysed or regard analysis with a certain confi-

---

[1] This guidance offers other advantages to the analyst as well. It makes the application of Ferenczi's "active therapy" possible, the suppression of individual symptoms, which then go to dam up libido so that more abundant material should be brought up into analysis.

dence and respect. Only so can the transition from the period of treatment back to home education be accomplished without a break. Where a child's analysis cannot be organically grafted onto the rest of its life, but is intruded like a disturbing foreign body into its other relationships, more conflicts for the child may be created than can be resolved by the treatment. This, I am afraid, is another disappointment.

But after telling you so much about the limitations of the analysis of children, I should not like to close without saying something of the considerable possibilities which it seems to me to hold, in spite of all its difficulties, and even with some advantage over the analysis of adults. I will suggest three of these.

We can bring about quite other modifications of character in the child than in the adult. The child, who under the influence of its neurosis has started out on the path of an abnormal character-development, need only retrace its steps a short distance in order to find the road which is normal and suited to its nature. It has not like the adult built up its whole life, chosen its calling, made friends, fallen in love, chosen its ideals, all on the basis of its neurotic tendencies. In the "character-analysis" of an adult we must actually shatter his whole life, and achieve the impossible, that is undo things already done, and not only make ignored mental processes conscious but abolish them altogether—if we wish for real success. Here the analysis of children has an infinite advantage.

The second possibility concerns influence upon the Super-ego. The moderation of its severity is, as you know, one of the purposes of the analysis. Here adult analysis encounters the greatest difficulties, for it has to contend with the individual's oldest and most important love-objects, his parents, which he has introjected through identification, and the memory of which is protected by filial piety. But in children's cases we have to do with living persons, existing in the outer world and not enshrined in memory. When we supplement internal work by external, and seek to modify, not only the existing identifications by analysis, but their actual prototypes by ordinary efforts, the result is both impressive and surprising.

The same is true for the third point. In working with an adult we have to confine ourselves entirely to helping him to adapt himself to his environment. It is far from us, and in fact lies quite outside our intention or our means, to shape his surroundings to meet his needs. But with a child we can do just this without any great difficulty. A child's needs are simpler and easier to fulfill and to oversee; our powers, combined with those of the parents, easily suffice under favourable conditions to provide for the child just what it requires, or much of it, at every stage of its treatment and progressive development. Thus we lighten the child's task of adjustment as we endeavour to adjust its surroundings. Here again is a double work, from within and from without.

I believe that it is due to these three factors that in the analysis of children, in spite of all the difficulties I have recounted, we can aim at transformations, improvements, and recoveries which are not even to be dreamt of in the analysis of adults.

Ladies and Gentlemen! I am prepared for the practising analysts among you to say, after what they have heard here, that my methods with children are so different that they cannot be called real analysis at all, but a form of "wild" analysis which has borrowed all its expedients from analysis but nowise conforms to strict analytical principles. But consider: If an adult neurotic came to your consulting room to ask for treatment, and on closer examination proved as impulsive, as undeveloped intellectually, and as deeply dependent on his

environment as are my child patients, you would probably say, "Freudian analysis is a fine method, but it is
not designed for such people." And you would treat the
patient by a mixed method, giving him as much pure
analysis as he can stand and for the rest children's analysis—because, owing to his infantile nature, he would
merit nothing better.

In my opinion, there can be no detraction to the
analytical method, designed as it is for a single particular
object, the adult neurotic, if one seeks to apply it with
modifications to other sorts of object. There is no harm
in contriving to use it for other purposes. Only one
should be at pains to know what one is doing.

PART II

The Theory of Children's Analysis
(1927)

THE THEORY OF CHILDREN'S ANALYSIS

Ladies and Gentlemen. In recent years the psycho-analysis of children has attracted greatly increased interest. This is mainly due to three factors. It brings welcome confirmation of the conceptions as to the mental life of children which psychoanalytical theory has formulated from adult analysis over the course of years; it supplies new disclosures to round out these ideas from direct observation; and finally it furnishes a transition to a sphere of application which, as many think, should in the future be one of the most important for psycho-analysis: to pedagogics, or the science of upbringing and education.

But, supported by these three claims to be of service, the analysis of children presumes to take various liberties. It calls for a new technique. There can be no real objection to this, for even the most conservative will admit that altered problems must be attacked by modified methods. And so there emerges Melanie Klein's play-technique for small children, and later the ideas propounded by me for analysis of the latency period. But some exponents of the analysis of children, and I among them, go even further. They are beginning to concern themselves with reflections as to whether the processes in a child's analysis are fully in accordance with those in an adult's, and whether the two fully coincide, so far as aim and end are concerned. They think that the children's analyst, just because the patient is a child, should have besides the analytical schooling and outlook a second—the educational. I do not see why we should be frightened of this word, or regard such a compound of two attitudes as a disparagement of analysis. It will be worth while to test the validity of this view in the light of some examples.

My first instance is from the analysis of an eleven-year-old boy. When the treatment began he was of the feminine-masochistic type, his original object-relationship with his mother being entirely overlaid by identification with her. His original masculine aggressiveness found relief only occasionally in hostile manifestations towards his brothers and sisters and delinquent acts, which were followed by violent fits of repentance and depression. In this period of his analysis he was preoccupied, in numerous ideas, fantasies and dreams, with the problem of death, or rather of the infliction of death.

At that time one of his mother's closest friends was very ill, and one day his mother received a telegram saying that her condition was dangerous. He seized on this for an elaborate daydream. He pretended that a fresh telegram arrived saying she was dead. His mother was extremely grieved. Then came another telegram—she is still alive, it was a mistake. The mother rejoiced. And then he fancied telegrams arriving in quick succession, always an announcement of death followed by another of revival. The fantasy ended with the news that the whole thing was a joke which someone had played on the mother. It is not difficult to interpret; we see his ambivalence clearly expressed, the wish to kill the person loved by his mother, and the inability to pursue his idea to its real conclusion.

Shortly after that, he reported to me the following compulsive action. When he sat in the lavatory he had to touch a knob which he found in the wall at one side three times with his hand; but then he had to repeat the process at once with a knob on the other side. This action seemed at first unintelligible, until the explanation was found next day through a fantasy recounted in another connection. He imagined God as an old man, seated in the heavenly abode on a great throne. To right and left of him were knobs or switches protruding from the wall. If he pressed the knobs on one side, someone died; if he pressed one on the other a child came into the world. I think the combination of the compulsive action with the daydream makes further interpretation superfluous. The number three is probably to be explained by the number of his brothers and sisters.

Soon afterwards the father of one of the boy's playfellows, who was a great friend of his mother, fell ill. The boy heard the telephone ring just as he was leaving for his appointment with me, and, while with me, constructed the following fantasy: His mother had been told that she must go to the invalid's house; she went there, entered the sickroom, went up to the bed and wished to talk with the patient. But he made no reply, and she saw that he was dead. It was a great shock to her. At that moment the dead man's little son came in. She called him and said "Come here, look, your father is dead." The boy came up to the bed and spoke to his father. The father was alive and answered him. He turned to my patient's mother and said "What is the matter? He is alive." Then she spoke again to the father, but again he made no reply and was dead. But when the boy came up again and spoke, the father was alive again.

This fantasy is instructive and transparent, and contains the interpretation of both the previous ones. We remark that the father is dead in his relationship to the mother, but alive so far as concerns his relations with the son. While in the previous fantasies the ambivalence —the wish to kill and to bring to life again—comprised merely two different reactions towards the same person, which must cancel each other out, in this one the particularisation of the threatened person (as man on the one hand and father on the other) gives the historical elucidation of the double attitude. The two impulses clearly spring from different phases of the boy's development. The death-wish against the father as the rival for the mother's love derives from the normal Oepidus phase with its since-repressed positive object-love for the mother. Here his masculine aggression turns against the father; he must be eliminated, to leave the way free for himself. But the other impulse, the wish to retain the father, comes on the one hand from the early period of the purely admiring and loving attitude to the father, undisturbed as yet by the rivalry of the Oedipus complex; and on the other hand from the phase—which here plays the more important part—of identification with the mother, which had replaced the normal Oedipus attitude. Through fear of castration, threatening from the father, the boy had surrendered his love for the mother and allowed himself to be forced into the feminine attitude. From then on he had to try to sustain the father as object of his homosexual love.

It would be tempting to go further, and describe the transition in the boy from this wish to kill to a fear of death which manifested itself each evening; and so to find a key to the complicated structure of this neurosis of the latency period. But that is no part of my present purpose. I have only mentioned this fragment to show that this part of the analysis of a child differs in no wise from that of an adult. We have to free a part of this boy's masculine aggressiveness from repression, and from the overlay of his present feminine-masochistic character and mother-identification. The conflict involved is an inner one. The fear of his real father in the outer world originally drove him into carrying out the repression, but the success of this achievement depends for its maintenance upon inner forces. The father has been "introjected," the Super-ego has become the representative of his power, and the fear of him is felt by the boy as castration anxiety. At every step which the analysis takes

on the path towards making conscious the repressed
Oedipus tendencies, it encounters outbreaks of this castration anxiety as an obstacle. Only the laborious histori-
co-analytical dissolution of this Super-ego will permit an
advance in my work of liberation. The work and attitude
of the treatment are, so far as this part of the problem is
concerned, purely analytical. There is no place here for
an educational admixture.

But in contrast listen to another example from the
analysis of the six-year-old obsessional little girl. Here
again, it is a matter of the impulses of the Oedipus complex, and here again the idea of killing plays a part. The
little girl had, as the analysis disclosed, gone through a
time of early passionate love for her father, and in the
usual way had been disappointed in him by the birth
of the next child. Her reaction to that was extraordi-
narily strong. She surrendered the barely achieved genital phase in favour of a full regression to anal sadism. She
turned her hostility against the new arrival. She made
an effort, having turned her love almost completely
away from her father, at least to retain him by incorpora-
tion. But her endeavours to feel herself a man struck
upon the rivalry with an elder brother, whom she recognised to be better equipped bodily for this rôle. The
result was an intensified hostility towards the mother
—hatred of her, because she had taken the father from
her; hatred, because she had not made her a boy; and
finally hatred, because she had borne the child whom my
little patient herself would willingly have brought into
the world. But at this point—somewhere in her fourth
year—something decisive occurred. She perceived dimly
that she was on the way to losing through these hate-
reactions, the loving relationship which from early childhood she had enjoyed with her still dearly-loved mother.
And in order to rescue her love for her mother, and still
more her own position of being loved by her, she made

a mighty effort to be "good." She split off, as it were with one stroke, all these hatreds, and with them her whole sexual life with its anal and sadistic habits and fantasies; and set this over against her own personality as something foreign to it, no longer native, something "devilish." What was left behind was not much: a small and limited person, whose emotional life was not fully at her disposal, and whose great intelligence and energy were occupied in holding the "devil" beneath the repression placed on it. For the outside world, she had at best only lukewarm feelings of tenderness towards her mother, not strong enough to bear even the slightest strain, and otherwise an almost complete lack of interest. But even so the devil occasionally overpowered her for a short time, so that it might happen that without any real occasion (externally) she would throw herself down on the ground and shriek, in a fashion which earlier would certainly have been dubbed possessed; or she would suddenly yield and revel with full satisfaction in sadistic fantasies, imagining that she wandered through her parents' house from top to bottom smashing all that she found and throwing the pieces out of the window, and striking off the heads of all the people she met. Such victories of the devil were always followed by anxiety and remorse. But the split-off evil had yet another way of manifesting itself, even more dangerous. The "devil" liked excrement and dirt; she herself began gradually to develop a particular anxiety as to the punctilious observance of the precepts of cleanliness. Beheading was a matter dear to the devil's heart; she then at a certain time in the morning must creep to the beds of her brothers and sisters to ascertain whether they were all still alive. The devil transgressed every human law with energy and relish; she however developed a fear of earthquake which came on in the evenings before going to sleep—for someone had given her the idea that earthquakes are the most effective means God uses to punish people on the earth. So in everyday life she engrossed herself more and more with reaction formations, acts of contrition, and reparation for the deeds of the split-off wickedness. The mighty and urgent effort, to retain her mother's love and to be socially conformable and "good," had come lamentably to grief; it had simply resulted in a compulsion-neurosis.

But I have not claimed your attention for this infantile neurosis because of its fine structure and the unusual sharpness, for this early age, with which the symptoms are circumscribed. I have described it because of a particular circumstance which emerged during the therapeutical work.

In the previous example the motor force of the repression was castration-anxiety relating to the father; naturally this operated as the main resistance in the analysis. But the analysis of the little girl worked differently. The repression or rather the splitting of the child's personality had come into being under the pressure of anxiety as to loss of love. The anxiety must have been very intense, to have such a disturbing effect on the child's whole life. But in this case this motivating anxiety did not operate in the analysis as a serious resistance. Under the effect of my uniform friendly interest the little patient began to disclose her "bad" side to me quite calmly and naturally. You may think that that was nothing out of the way. Often enough we meet adult patients who anxiously conceal their symptoms from the world, and only begin to disclose them in the secure and uncriticising atmosphere of analysis; who, indeed, often only recognise them there for the first time. But this only refers to the description of the symptoms; the friendly interest and absence of expected criticism never suffice to induce alteration of them. This however was just what happened here. When to my interest and lack of condemnation there was added a relaxation of the strict home discipline, there suddenly occurred a change of anxiety into the wish concealed beneath it, of a reaction-formation into the rejected instinct, and of a precaution into the underlying death-threat. The anxiety as to loss of love, which should have opposed itself in violent outbreaks to such a situation, was hardly manifest at all. The resistance from that cause was slighter than from any other. It was as though the little girl were saying "If you do not think it so bad, then I do not either." And with this diminution of her own demands on herself she gradually accomplished, in the course of the analysis, a progressive reincorporation of all the impulses which previously she had put away with such expenditure of effort: the incestuous love for her father, the wish to be masculine, the death-wishes against brothers and sisters, the acknowledgement of her childish sexuality; and only paused with the single serious resistance for a time before what seemed to her the worst of all, the acknowledgement of the direct death-wish against her mother.

That is not the behaviour which we have learned to expect from a Super-ego. We have learned from the adult neurotic how inaccessible to reason the Super-ego is, how steadfastly it resists every attempt at external influence, and how it will not consent to modify its demands until we have historically dissected it in analysis and traced back every single command and prohibition to the identification with one of the persons who loomed large and were loved in childhood.

I believe that we have come here upon the main and most important difference between the analysis of adults and that of children. Take the situation in adult analysis, where the Super-ego has already achieved its independence. Here our sole task is to raise all the impulses deriving from the Id, the Ego and the Super-ego, which partook in the formation of the neurotic conflict, to the same level by bringing them into consciousness. On this new conscious level the conflict can then be carried on in a new way and brought to another outcome. But in the analysis of children we deal with cases where the Super-ego has not yet arrived at any real independence; where it operates all too clearly for the sake of those from whom it holds its commission, the parents and persons in charge of the child, and is swayed in its demands by every change in the relationship with these people and by all the alterations that may occur in their own outlook. We work, as with adults, by pure analysis, in so far as it is a matter of freeing the already repressed part of the Id and the Ego. But the task with the childish Super-ego is a double one. It is analytical in the historical dissolution of the Super-ego, so far as it is already an independent structure, from within, but it is also educational (in the widest sense of that word) in exercising outward influence, by modifying the relations with those who are bringing up the child, creating new impressions, and revising the demands made on the child by the outside world.

To return to my little obsessional patient. Had she not come under treatment at six-year-old her infantile neurosis might perhaps, like so many others, have cleared up of itself. As heir to it a strict Super-ego would certainly have been raised up, which would have presented rigid demands to the Ego and would have opposed to any later analysis a resistance difficult to overcome. But the view which I put forward is that this strict Super-ego stands at the outcome and not at the inception of the infantile neurosis.

As a further illustration of what I have said I refer to a communication which Dr. M. W. Wulff has published (73). He reports phobic attacks of anxiety in a little girl aged only one and a half. Clearly in this case the child's parents had tried too early to make it form habits of cleanliness. The little child could not come up to their requirements and became upset, imagining that she would be sent away. Her anxiety became acute in the dark or when there were sounds, for instance if someone knocked at the door. She constantly asked whether she was good and kept repeating the plea not to be sent away. The worried parents turned to Dr. Wulff for advice.

The interesting point about this early symptom is that the infant's anxiety, which Dr. Wulff at once recognised as fear of loss of love, is in no way distinguishable from the guilt-feelings of an adult neurotic. Must we however in this case give credence to so early a development of conscience, and thus of the Super-ego?

Dr. Wulff explained to the parents that the little girl clearly could not yet for some reason carry out the requirements of cleanliness, and advised them to postpone for a time her education in this respect. They were understanding enough to comply; they explained to the child that they still loved her when she wetted herself, and they tried whenever that happened to allay her fears with renewed reassurances. The result as Dr. Wulff described it was striking. After a few days the child was calm and free from anxiety.

Such "therapy" is naturally only possible very seldom and with very small children. I do not want to suggest that it is the only possible one. But Dr. Wulff has here afforded a proof by cure, which permits a positive conclusion as to the play of forces at the root of the anxiety. If the child's anxiety had been due to the Super-ego's demands, the parents' reassurances would have had hardly any influence on her symptom. If however the cause of her anxiety was the real fear of the displeasure of her parents, actually existing in the outside world, and not of an inward image of them, then it is easily to be understood that the symptom could be removed. Dr. Wulff had in fact removed its cause.

The Super-ego's accessibility to influence in early years accounts for many of the direct modifications which can be brought about in a young child's behaviour. Through the good offices of Dr. Ferenczi, I have had access to the notes of a teacher in a modern American school, the Walden School. She describes how neurotic children from strict homes, who come to school while still of kindergarten age, after a first period of surprise and suspicion become acclimatised to the free atmosphere and gradually lose their neurotic symptoms, which are usually reactions to the breaking off of masturbation. A similar result would be impossible in the case of an adult neurotic. The freer the surroundings into which he is transplanted, the stronger his anxiety in respect of the instinct, and the stronger his neurotic defence reactions, i.e. his symptoms. The demands which his Super-ego lays upon him are no longer open to influence from his surroundings. On the other hand, the child, when the mitigation of its Super-ego's demands once has begun, is apt to go to extremes, and to indulge itself further than even the freest environment is ready to permit. The exercise of external influence is again necessary.

In conclusion, one more example. A little while ago I overheard a conversation between a five-year-old boy and his mother. The child had taken the fancy to wish for a live horse; his mother on good grounds opposed the fulfilment of this desire. "It doesn't matter," said he, not at all cast down, "I'll wish for it for my next birthday." His mother told him that even then he could not have it. "Then I'll wish for it at Christmas," he said, "one gets anything then." "No, not even at Christmas," said his mother, trying to disabuse him. "Well it still doesn't matter," said he triumphantly, "I shall buy it myself, *for I allow myself to have it*." This is a clear illustration of the conflict which arises when an inner permission is confronted by a prohibition from without. If they are fortunate, children will adapt themselves to frustration; if not, the outcome may be rebellion and delinquency, or neurosis.

Yet one word more on the "educational" function of the children's analyst. Since we have found that the forces with which we have to contend in the cure of an infantile neurosis are not only internal, but partly external as well, we have a right to require that the children's analyst should correctly assess the external situation in which the child stands; just as we ask that he should measure and comprehend its inner situation. For this part of his task however the children's analyst needs theoretical and practical knowledge of children's training and upbringing. This enables him to look into and criticise the educational influence under which the child is being brought up; and, if it should prove necessary, to take the child's upbringing out of the hands of those in charge, and for the period of the analysis undertake it himself.

PART III

Indications for Child Analysis
(1945)

INTRODUCTION

Since 1905, when a phobia in a five-year-old boy was first treated by psychoanalysis—the father acting as intermediary between child and analyst—child analysis as a therapeutic method has had a stormy and much chequered career (74). There is hardly a point in it which has remained uncontested, or which has not, at some time or other, become the starting-point for controversy.

In some respects child-analysis revived the same objections which the psychoanalytic treatment of adults had to meet and overcome a full decade earlier.

1. THE SEXUAL PREJUDICE

At the end of the last century the conception of a sexual origin of adult neurosis ran counter to all the prejudices of that age. But, though medical and lay opinion would not concede to adult sexuality the pathogenic importance which it deserved, no one went so far as to deny its existence altogether; everybody on the other hand violently objected to the possible existence of a sexual life in childhood. Psychoanalysis had laid itself open to the reproach of over-estimating the role of sexuality in the adult, and, similarly, to a charge of inventing an infantile sex life, contrary to the facts then known and accepted by the medical world and in educational circles. Thus the existence of an infantile sexuality had to be established and proved at the same time as the rôle of such a sexual life for the neuroses of childhood had to be demonstrated (75).

2. THE FEAR OF IMMORALITY AS A CONSEQUENCE
OF PSYCHOANALYTIC TREATMENT

A second argument which was originally used against the analytic treatment of adult neurotics was based on a misconception of the psychoanalytic process itself. It was thought that the constant preoccupation with instinctive tendencies which is inherent in the analytic work, the release of these tendencies from repression, and their consequent rising up to consciousness could have one effect only: their expression in actions, i.e. the fulfilment of the instinctive (sexual and aggressive) wishes which had been kept under restraint before the treatment. Psychoanalytical treatment would thus lead directly to immorality and licentiousness. It had needed much patient and lengthy demonstration to convince the public that this was not the case; that, on the contrary, far from becoming more potent, unconscious tendencies were deprived of most of their power when an outlet into conscious thought was opened up for them. Relegated to the unconscious these instinctive urges had been out of reach; unearthed, and lifted to the conscious level they automatically came under the control of the patient's mind and could be dealt with according to his ideas and ideals.

The same objections which had been successfully refuted with regard to adult patients rose up again in full force when child-analysis made its first appearance. The argument was this time that surely the childish mind could not be trusted with the same discretion in dealing with its reawakened instinctive tendencies as the adult one. Surely the child would want to make full use of the licence offered to it in the analytic situation and give free rein to its instinctive urges inside and outside of the analytic hour. Or even if its intentions were otherwise, its attempts at restraint and adapted behaviour would be simply overrun by the instinctive forces let loose through the agency of analytic treatment. Fears of this kind were expressed not only by doctors, teachers and parents, but were shared to a degree by some analysts who thought it quite possible that child-analysis might need some special form of educational guidance as its constant accompaniment and counterpart. But, as experience proved, this was not as often necessary as had been expected. It was demonstrated repeatedly that the ego and super-ego of a child which were consistent and severe enough to produce an infantile neurosis could also, with some help, be relied on to deal with the sexual and aggressive impulses which emerged from repression after the neurosis had been analysed successfully. Fears of this nature are more justified where the object of child-analysis is not a neurotic, but a dissocial, delinquent, or otherwise deficient character.

3. CONTROVERSIES ABOUT THE TECHNIQUE
   OF CHILD-ANALYSIS

It became obvious immediately that the classical analytical technique was not applicable to children, at least not before the age of puberty, or at best pre-puberty. Free association, the mainstay of analytic technique, had to be counted out as a method; young children are neither willing nor able to embark on it. This has its consequences for the second main road to the unconscious, namely dream-interpretation. Children tell their dreams freely; but without the use of free association the interpretation of the manifest dream content is less fruitful and convincing. The child-analyst frequently has to supply the links between the manifest dream content and the latent dream thoughts according to his own intimate knowledge of the child's inner situation at the time of dreaming. It is, further, impossible to establish the same outward setting for the analytic hour. Children cannot be placed on the analytic couch for the purpose of relaxed concentration without this having the effect of silencing them completely. Talk and action cannot be separated from each other in their case. Nor can the patient's family be wholly excluded from the analysis. Insight into the seriousness of the neurosis, the decision to begin and to continue treatment, persistence in the face of resistance or of passing aggravations of the illness are beyond the child, and have to be supplied by the parents. In child-analysis the parents' good sense plays the part which the healthy part of the patient's conscious personality plays during adult analysis to safeguard and maintain the continuance of treatment.

To establish techniques which were adapted to the varying needs of the different phases of childhood, it became above all necessary to create appropriate substitutes for free association. The first divergence of opinion between child-analysts arose about this matter. Certain child-analysts (Hug-Hellmuth in Vienna, Melanie Klein in Berlin and later in London) developed the so-called play technique of child-analysis, a method which promised to give more or less direct access to the child's unconscious. In this technique, for free association was substituted the spontaneous play-activity of the child, carried out on small toy material which was offered by the analyst for free use within the analytic hour. The individual actions of the child in connection with this material were considered to be equivalent to the individual thoughts or images in a chain of free association. In this manner the production of material for interpretation became largely independent of the child's willingness or ability to express itself in speech.

Other child-analysts (on the European continent and in the United States) were reluctant to employ this play technique to the same extent. This method of interpretation, though allowing as if in flashes a certain amount of direct insight into the child's unconscious, seemed to them to be open to objections of various kinds. Like all interpretation of symbols (for instance purely symbolical dream-interpretation) it has a tendency to become rigid, impersonal and stereotyped without being open to corroboration from the child; it aimed at laying bare the deeper layers of the child's mind without working through the resistances and distortions of the preconscious and of consciousness. Furthermore they refused to accept these activities as real equivalents of free association. The free associations of the adult patient are produced in the set situation of analytic transference and, though freed from the usual restrictions of logical and conscious thought, are under the influence of one governing aim; that of being cured by analysis. The play activity of the child is not governed by any similar intention. This leads to the further, open and controversial question whether the relationship of the child to the analyst is really governed exclusively by a transference situation. Even if one part of the child's neurosis is transformed into a transference neurosis, in the manner in which this happens in adult analysis, another part of the child's neurotic reactions remains grouped around the parents who are the original objects of the pathogenic past. It was due to considerations of this nature that a large number of child-analysts evolved techniques of a different kind. They worked on the various derivatives of the child's unconscious in day- and night-dreams, in imaginative play, in drawings, etc., including the emotional reactions of the child, inside and outside of the analytic hour. The task was, as in adult analysis, to undo the various repressions, distortions, displacements, condensations, etc., which had been brought about by the neurotic defence-mechanisms, until, with the active help of the child, the unconscious content of the material was laid bare. Such co-operation with the child naturally presupposes the extensive use of speech.

Detailed accounts of the two different types of child-analysis are contained in Melanie Klein's *The Psycho-Analysis of Children* (5), and in my *Introduction to the Technique of the Analysis of Children* (4).

The method of symbolic interpretation of play activity which Melanie Klein had devised for her technique was later taken over by psychotherapy and widely used in England and America under the name of "play-therapy." But in these instances it was deprived of its full original meaning, since it was used without reference to an analytical transference situation.

4. CONTROVERSIES CONCERNING THE APPROPRIATE AGE FOR CHILD-ANALYSIS

Differences in the manner in which child-analysis was carried out inevitably led to differences concerning the age at which the therapeutic method was applicable. The decisive factor in this respect was the use of speech. Melanie Klein and her followers repeatedly expressed the opinion that, with the help of the play technique, children can be analysed at almost any age, from earliest infancy onwards. When the faculty of speech in the child is of major importance for the treatment, it is hardly possible to contemplate analysis before the age of two or three. The majority of cases treated with these latter techniques were considerably older than that; many of them were analysed at the height of the Oedipus complex (four or five years), or in the latency period.

5. CONTROVERSIES CONCERNING THE RANGE OF APPLICA-
TION OF CHILD-ANALYSIS

Here again a wide difference of opinion exists between the school of Melanie Klein and the former
Vienna school of child-analysts, many of whom are at
present working in America. The English child-analysts
express the view that every child passes in its infancy
through phases of grave abnormality (psychotic states,
depressions, etc.), and that normal development in later
stages can best be safeguarded by early child-analysis,
by analysing the psychotic residues of the earliest stage
whenever outward circumstances permit. The former
Vienna school on the other hand is of the opinion that
the application of child-analysis may well be restricted
to the most severe cases of the infantile neurosis through
which every child normally passes at one time or other
before entering the latency period. With all other children, the application of analytical knowledge to their
educational handling may prove sufficient to guide them
through the intricacies of their instinctual and emotional development.

THE EVALUATION OF INFANTILE NEUROSES

1. SELECTION OF CASES

Those who do not share the opinion that analysis
should be universally applied to all children are faced
with the task of selecting their cases, that is, of assessing
the seriousness of the various manifestations of infantile
neurosis. In practice child-analysts of to-day have little
opportunity of determining this matter by their own
judgment. The question whether or not a child should
be analysed is usually decided for them, and frequently
enough on inadequate reasons. Children who are se-

verely ill are often withheld from treatment because their parents, with whom the decision lies, know too little about analysis, or are frightened of the little which they know; because the parents are reluctant to have the intimacies of their own lives exposed to the analyst; because they fear the sexual enlightenment of the child; because they, especially the mothers, are unwilling to see a stranger succeed with their child where they themselves have failed. Sometimes the reasons given are very superficial: analytic hours would clash with school hours; would take up the time otherwise given to sport or handicraft, or some other occupation, from which the child usually has ceased to benefit owing to its neurotic disturbance. The most decisive factor is frequently the geographical one. To accompany a child to and from a daily analytical hour is a heavy burden on the mother; where long distances aggravate the issue, this factor is often prohibitive.

On the other hand, a number of children are sent into analysis, not because they suffer from an excessive form of infantile neurosis, but because their parents, either as analytic patients themselves, or as practising analysts, are more apt than others to detect and evaluate signs of neurotic behaviour whenever they appear. They readily decide for analytic treatment at an early stage to avoid for their child the graver forms of neurotic suffering which they know only too well from personal experience. Their positive decision for treatment, like the above mentioned negative ones, is based rather on a personal attitude than on an objective assessment of the child's disturbance.

The child cases actually in treatment in our day, either in child departments of the psychoanalytic clinics or in private practice, are thus a more or less chance selection, not a representative selection of infantile neuroses which are most in need of therapeutic help. It is to be expected that these conditions will change when knowledge about the mental development of the young child becomes more widespread, that is, when parents understand at least as much about the importance of instinctual, emotional or intellectual setbacks in the child's development as they understand now about its bodily illnesses. The assessment of the disturbance and the decision whether treatment is indicated or not will then be left to the psychologist or psychoanalyst, as it is nowadays left to the pediatrician in all cases of organic disturbance.

(a) *The factor of neurotic suffering*

The question whether or not an adult neurotic seeks treatment is in the last resort dependant on the amount of suffering which his neurotic symptoms cause him. For this reason neurotics undergo treatment more willingly than for instance, perverts. A perversion disrupts normal life as much as a neurosis. But the perversion brings satisfaction whereas neurotic symptoms are painful.

This statement can be upheld in spite of the fact that every neurosis is also a source of pleasure for the individual who is afflicted by it. The pleasure which the patient derives from the distorted gratification of repressed wishes, that is from his symptoms, is not experienced as pleasure by his conscious system. The conscious pleasure, on the other hand, which neurotics often enjoy owing to the consideration which they receive from their environment, a sense of importance, etc., is of a secondary nature and not really inherent in the illness. Whenever this secondary gain from the illness becomes greater than the neurotic suffering itself, the patient will be unfit for treatment, or will in most cases quite openly refuse to be treated. The existence of neurotic suffering is, if not indispensable, at least an important prerequisite for the attitude of persistence and determination which a patient needs to carry him through the difficulties of an analytic cure.

In dealing with cases of infantile neurosis one realises that neurotic suffering is not present in the child to the same degree, and that, wherever it is present, it is equally divided between child and parents. In some instances it is only the reaction of the parents to the symptom which, secondarily, brings home to the child that it suffers from a symptom. This is for instance the case in the frequent feeding disturbances of childhood. Children become bad eaters for reasons which originate in their early mother-relationship, in their reactions against their oral-sadistic and their anal-sadistic tendencies, etc. The normal intake of food is thus made difficult or impossible for neurotic reasons. The child, left to itself, would gladly put up with this symptom and eat less. Mothers, on the other hand, suffer acutely from anxiety caused by this behaviour of the child and, in their turn, inflict suffering on the bad eater through reproaches, scoldings, forcible measures, etc. The same occurs in the neurotic bed-wetting of childhood. Children under a certain age tend to show indifference towards this symptom while the adult environment suffers badly on its account; the amount of pain which it causes the child depends on the reaction of the environment. The night terrors of children (pavor nocturnus) usually cause consternation and anxiety to the parents while the afflicted child itself remains oblivious of them. Temper tantrums are disturbing for the family; for the child itself they are often a welcome outlet. Neurotic display of aggression and destructiveness, as they occur in the initial stages of an obsessional neurosis, are most disturbing symptoms for the family; the child rather indulges in them. Its attitude in that respect resembles more closely that of an adult pervert than of an adult neurotic.

Acute neurotic suffering is felt by the child in all states of anxiety before a consistent defence against it has set in. When anxiety is once warded off, either by phobic or by obsessional mechanisms, how much the child suffers depends again on the behaviour of the environment. Many mothers fear the child's anxiety as much as the child does himself. Consequently they not only do not oppose the child's phobic or obsessional arrangements, they even help actively and in many ways to uphold them. They help the child to avoid the danger situations in which anxiety would arise; they fall in with bed-time ceremonials, with eating, dressing and washing obsessions, etc. Their object is to spare the child the suffering inherent in the anxiety, and simultaneously to avoid the violent outbreaks which follow whenever an obsessional act or phobic precaution is opposed or prevented. There are thus many infantile phobias and obsessional neuroses which exist under the surface and, though causing endless trouble for the mother, are not felt as acutely painful by the child.

(During the time of mass evacuation in England, 1940, many children became neurotic sufferers after separation from their parents. It would be erroneous to conclude that they had acquired a neurosis due to their traumatic experiences. In many cases their neurosis had merely not been in evidence while they lived with their mothers, and acute anxiety, suffering, etc., appeared when they had to live with people who were less willing or able to show consideration for their phobic and obsessional arrangements.)

To sum up: the presence or absence of suffering cannot be counted on as a decisive factor when making up one's mind about the treatment of a child. There are many serious neurotic disorders which the child bears with equanimity; there are less serious ones which cause pain. Since the decision to seek advice for the child normally lies with the parents, an infantile neurosis is more likely to come into treatment when its symptoms are disturbing to the environment. The parents will be guided in their assessment of the seriousness of the situation by the impact of the child's neurosis on themselves. They show more concern, for instance, about aggressive and destructive states than about inhibitions; obsessional acts are taken more lightly than anxiety attacks, though in reality they represent a more advanced stage of the same disorder; bed-wetters are taken to clinics more regularly than any other category of cases; the beginning stages of passive femininity in young boys, though often decisive for their whole future abnormality, are almost invariably overlooked.

(b) *The factor of disturbance of normal capacities*

An adult neurosis is not only assessed subjectively according to suffering, but objectively according to the extent to which it damages the main capacities of the individual: the capacity to lead a normal love and sex life, and the capacity to work. Patients usually decide to come into treatment when one or the other of these functions, or both, are severely threatened.

The question arises whether there are any functions in the child's life, the disturbance of which is an equally significant indicator for the seriousness of the infantile neurosis.

The child's love and sex life is, as psychoanalysis has shown, not less extensive and certainly not less intensive than that of the adult. But, after the first severe repressions of early childhood have occurred, it is inhibited in its aims. Though centred according to objects (Oedipus complex), it is diffuse in its manifestations (component instincts), not organised under the primacy of any single one of them. It furthermore lacks a climax in its expressions, the disturbance of which could be taken as indicative of disturbance of function. The child is, according to the nature of its sex organisation, impotent, which means that the intactness of its sexuality is more difficult to gauge than with an adult. To measure its capacity for object-love we can only measure its libidinal urges directed towards the outer world against its narcissistic tendencies. Normally after the first year of life object love should outweigh narcissism; satisfaction derived from objects should become increasingly greater than autoerotic gratification. An infantile neurosis can seriously interfere with these proportions. But the assessment of these factors in the diagnosis is too subtle and too complicated to be of immediate help as an indication for treatment.

It is equally difficult to find in the child's life a parallel for the disturbance of working capacity. It has been suggested by many authors that play is as important for the child as work is for the adult, and that consequently a test of the child's ability to play is highly suggestive for the extent of its disturbance. This view seems to be borne out by the fact that neurotic children are invariably disturbed in their play activity. With certain types of neurosis imaginative play is excessive, at the expense of constructive play. In its initial stages this is sometimes taken as an asset by the parents, as the sign of a specially vivid imagination and of artistic gifts. But the neurotic element is unmistakable when such play becomes repetitive, monotonous, and interferes with all other kinds of activity. This should be taken as a sign that the child is neurotically fixed to a certain point of its libidinal development.

Although the capacity for constructive play is, in the child's life, the nearest substitute for the adult capacity to work, the two functions remain so far removed from each other that it is hardly justifiable to give them an equal place in the diagnosis. Since play is governed by the pleasure principle, and work by the reality principle, the disturbance of each of the two functions has a different clinical significance.

(c) The factor of disturbance of normal development

It is thus impracticable to use for the evaluation of an infantile neurosis the same criteria which we apply in the case of an adult. Childhood is a process *sui generis,* a series of developmental stages in which each manifestation has its importance as a transition, not as a final result. Its tasks and accomplishments cannot therefore be compared with those of the more static stage of adulthood. There is only one factor in childhood which has such central importance that its impairment through a neurosis calls for immediate action: that is the child's ability to develop, not to remain fixed to any stage of development before a prescribed ripening process has been concluded. The suggestion is therefore to assess the seriousness of an infantile neurosis, not according to the damage which it does to the activities or attitudes of the child in any special way, or at any given moment, but according to the degree in which it prevents the child from developing further.

2. LIBIDINAL DEVELOPMENT

(a) The sequence of libidinal development

On the basis of our present knowledge it is possible, even in a cursory examination, to establish whether a child is up to its age in its libidinal development. We roughly know the age limits for the pregenital organisations of the libido, plus some subdivisions within these stages. Gross disturbance in the order of events, or failure to move on from any of these transitory stages in children who are neither organically nor mentally deficient, points to serious neurotic interference.

But wide individual variability, and the scantiness of our knowledge, prevent us from making anything beyond rough estimates on this basis. We have to count, normally, with an extensive overlapping between the various organisations. The oral phase, for instance, persists for months, after the anal-sadistic organisation has come into being; anal-sadistic manifestations do not disappear with the beginning of the phallic phase. The latency period is usually in existence for one or two years before the tendencies of the first infantile period fade into the background. It would, for instance, be erroneous to conclude from a continuance of oral or anal forms of auto-erotic gratification in the fourth or fifth years, that the child has failed to reach the phallic level. It never happens that the whole of the libido expresses itself in the manifestations of the latest phase of development only; some part of it invariably remains attached to earlier modes of expression. To ensure normality it is sufficient if the bulk of the libido reaches the organisation which is appropriate to the age of the child. The manifestations of this level then predominate over the earlier ones, though never as fully as the genital tendencies of adult sex life predominate over the pregenital tendencies.

There are more reliable data on which an opinion about the libidinal development of a child could, theoretically, be based: namely the fantasies which accompany the child's masturbatory activities. But, practically, this is of little help for the diagnosis. Such fantasies are always hidden, very frequently unconscious, and only laid bare in the course of an analysis, not in a consultation.

(b) *The intactness of libidinal development*

The libidinal normality of a child is, further, judged according to the fate of the individual component instincts. We would not expect any of the component instincts to be completely absent from the clinical picture (if the child is neither organically nor mentally deficient) except as a sign of severe neurotic disturbance.

But, again, individual variability is wide enough to warn us to be careful in our conclusions. The component instincts (including tendencies like exhibitionism, scoptophilia), or rather their manifestations, are not visible to the same degree in all children; nor does any individual child present us with equally clear pictures of all the different libidinal tendencies. Usually some of the component instincts are clearly in evidence, others remain faint and shadowy. With some children we might believe that cruelty, or exhibitionism, or greed, have played hardly any part in their lives; with others these urges are unmistakable, and other instincts are only seen on closer observation. Individual differences of this nature are based on constitutional factors, and are not due to neurotic interference; but they create points of special libidinal interests in the child's life, so-called fixation-points, which play an important rôle in later neurotic development.

(c) *Neurotic interference with libidinal development; the factor of spontaneous recovery*

A neurosis in an adult damages the intactness of the individual's sex-organisation; an infantile neurosis interferes besides this directly with the forward movement of the libido.

In the beginning stage of a neurotic conflict the

libido, to avoid anxiety which has arisen on a higher level of sex organisation, flows backwards (regression), and attaches itself once more to earlier libidinal wishes (fixation point). The ego of the child thus finds itself confronted with primitive desires (oral, aggressive, anal), which it is not prepared to tolerate. It defends itself against the instinctual danger with the help of various mechanisms (repression, reaction-formation, displacements, etc), but, if such defence is unsuccessful, neurotic symptoms arise which represent the gratification of the wish, distorted in its form by the action of the repressive forces. While these symptoms persist, they are the central expression of the child's libidinal life.

From the developmental point of view it is immaterial whether such symptoms are a little more or a little less painful. What counts is that with the onset of the neurotic disturbance the libido has been arrested in its course. Instead of moving on towards more adult levels, it has been forced backwards, and important gains have thereby been undone. Qualities and achievements which depend directly on the stage of libido development are lost. The child who regresses to the oral level, for instance, simultaneously reverts to the emotional attitudes which are connected with it: it becomes once more insatiable, exacting, impatient for wishfulfilment, "like a baby." Regression from the phallic to the anal-sadistic level destroys the hardly acquired attitudes of generosity, manliness and protectiveness and substitutes for them the domineering possessiveness which belongs to the earlier libidinal level. But progress is made at the same time in other spheres which are not influenced directly by the neurosis. The child grows bigger and more clever, and its development becomes inharmonious since this growing body and mind are tied to an instinctual and emotional life which cannot keep pace with it. The need for treatment seems urgent at this stage, not because the neurosis is in itself so severe, but because the presence of the neurosis hinders libido development.

On the other hand this impression of a serious hold-up is frequently misleading. After a shorter or a longer stay, symptoms may suddenly lose importance; the fixation can dissolve and the libido, freed from restrictions, resume its normal progressive flow. The child has, as the popular saying goes, "outgrown" its neurosis, and therapeutic help has become unnecessary.

As analysts, who collect their evidence from adult cases, we do not readily believe in the spontaneous cure of a neurosis, and we view such appearances with distrust when they are brought to our notice. We know that neuroses can, at best, change their manifestations. Neurotic anxiety for instance can disappear, but only to reappear later, centred round a different object or topic. Changes in life circumstances can alleviate a neurotic condition in various ways. Neurotic suffering can be exchanged for ordinary suffering; for instance the real loss of an object through death can take the place of the imagined loss of love from that object, and thus make a particular symptom unnecessary. A masochistic desire, which at one time manifests itself in neurotic symptoms, can find satisfaction in organic illness at another time. Inhibitions or obsessional restrictions which cripple a patient's activity may be given up when the same person is, for instance, in prison or in a concentration camp, that is, lives under crippling and inhibiting circumstances. A neurosis can further be relieved through separation from the love object on to which it has transferred its central issues; but such relief will be temporary, and the neurosis will soon re-establish itself completely when a new transference has taken place. Happenings of this kind, though often described as temporary or permanent spontaneous cures, are merely slight fluctuations within the neurotic arrangement itself.

On the basis of our theoretical knowledge, there is little reason to expect the neuroses of adults to clear up spontaneously. The neurotic symptom, as a compromise between two opposing forces, can only alter when decisive changes take place, either in the instinctive tendencies or in the ego and super-ego of the individual. Neither kind of change is likely to happen in the adult. The infantile wish, to which the patient has regressed, will remain potent. The ego will keep its repressive energy (unless a serious deteriorating process sets in). Furthermore, the whole process is anchored in the unconscious, and therefore not accessible to influence from conscious levels.

This is where conditions in the case of an infantile neurosis are completely different. The child's libido organisation is, as described before, in a fluid state, the libido moving on continuously towards new positions. A component instinct which is charged with libido in one phase, may be devoid of interest at another. The child need not remain hopelessly tied to any fixation-point to which it has been led back through regression. If the fixation is not excessively strong, the libido has a good chance of freeing itself again, carried forward by the next wave of development. This possibility is greatest at times when the biological urges are of especial strength, as they are at the onset of the phallic phase (four-five years) and of puberty.

(It is a common error to believe that, due to the strengthening of the ego, children become more neurotic in the latency period. On the contrary, the latency period marks a definite decrease in infantile neurosis. At that time the strength of the infantile sex wishes dies down, partly for biological reasons, partly owing to the frustration of the child's Oedipus wishes. This lessens the need for defence against the instincts and alters the compromise-formations between ego and id which lie at the root of symptom formation. Many infantile neuroses therefore disappear at approximately that date, their spontaneous cure being due to these quantitative changes.

Puberty is rightly regarded as a time when numerous neurotic disturbances may be expected to appear. It is less well known that puberty also removes certain neurotic symptoms which are typical for the years preceding it. This refers especially to the neurotic behaviour of boys who, all through early childhood and latency, fight against repressed wishes of a passive feminine kind. Their behaviour is characterised by anxiety, due to their repressed castration wishes, and by a superficial and noisy aggressiveness which is a reaction against the underlying passivity. Puberty brings a biological increase in genital masculinity which, while it lasts, puts the anal, passive and feminine tendencies out of action. This is a spontaneous cure in the real sense of the word: the neurosis not merely changes its form, but the underlying unconscious forces themselves undergo alterations. It depends on future developments whether the former constellation of instincts will come to the fore again in adult life; in this case the neurotic defence against it will be re-instated.

There are other typical examples of infantile neuroses which disappear almost invariably before adolescence: bed-wetting, and some of the common eating disturbances. They also are swept away by the libidinal changes before or in puberty. Certain disorders affecting sexual potency, and certain nervous disorders of the stomach may, much later, appear in their stead, if the adult genital sex organisation is not strong enough to maintain itself.)

To sum up: the decision whether a child needs therapeutic help or not can be based on the state of the libido development. An infantile neurosis can be treated as a transitory disorder so long as the libido organisation of the child remains fluid and shows progressive tendencies. Infantile neuroses disappear whenever the normal forward movement of the libido is strong enough to undo neurotic regression and fixation. When the libido constellations become rigid, stabilised, and monotonous in their expressions the neurosis is in danger of remaining permanently. This means that treatment is indicated.

This view, that child-analysis should be used sparingly, in cases where the hope for a spontaneous recovery is slight or non-existent, is opposed to the opinion which many analysts hold, that child-analysis might be used prophylactically, to remove the pathogenic fixation-points.

3. NEUROTIC INTERFERENCE WITH EGO-DEVELOPMENT

The threat which the occurrence of an infantile neurosis constitutes for the libido development of the individual is so blatant that it has not escaped notice. The same danger is less obvious where the development of the ego is concerned. On the contrary, there is a common belief that neurotic development in children is coupled with an especially good, frequently an especially early, blossoming of this side of the child's personality. It is left an open question whether it is the infantile neurosis which, as one of its results, overemphasizes the side of the ego forces, or whether it is an early ripening of the ego which predisposes the child for a severe infantile neurosis.

The following is an attempt to examine the questions whether a childhood neurosis helps or harms the building up of the ego; what the interactions are between the two processes; and whether the degree of harm done to the ego can serve as a further indication for the therapeutic use of child-analysis.

(a) *The quantitative factor in ego-development*

A neurosis can affect the ego quantitatively, that is, in its strength.

The term ego strength is not meant to denote an absolute quantity of ego forces which are, in themselves, not measurable. It refers to the relative efficiency of the ego with regard to the contents of the id (the instincts) and to the forces of the environment with which the ego has to deal. This ego strength varies repeatedly in the course of normal development. In the beginning of life the instincts are of overwhelming strength and the first crystallisations of an ego are completely under their domination and at their service. The child's growing awareness of the outside world, the beginnings of its ability to retain and connect memory traces, to foresee events, to draw conclusions from them, etc., are used exclusively for the purpose of instinct gratification. The better the ego development of an infant, the better are its chances to gratify its desires and to use the outside world for the fulfilment of its wishes. This undisputed reign of the instincts does not last longer than early infancy. As a result of its strong emotional ties to the parents, the child soon begins to regard their wishes, which are frequently in opposition to its own. To the degree in which it is able to identify with the parents who educate it, its ego develops hostile attitudes towards its instincts and attempts to oppose and manage them. Simultaneously it begins to correlate conflicting emotions and tendencies instead of giving alternate expression to them as has happened so far. This means suppressing one or the other side of them (love or hate, active or passive desires, etc.), and creates new conflicts between ego and id. But although all these efforts are made by the ego to assert itself against the instincts, no real ego superiority is established in the first period of childhood. The pull of wishfulfilment is still too strong, and the principle which governs the child's life remains to a large extent the pleasure principle. It is only the final frustration of the Oedipus wishes, with the consequent fading out of the early libido organisations, which changes the situation decisively in favour of ego strength. While the sex drives remain latent (latency period), the ego assumes superiority, directs the actions of the child, establishes the reality principle, and effects the first real adaptation to the exigencies of the outside world. Ego and id have now reversed their positions. But the new order is by no means permanent. Ego superiority is overthrown again as soon as the first signs of adolescence appear. Because of the biological increase in pre-genital tendencies during pre-puberty, and genital tendencies during puberty, the libidinal forces rise in strength. During the whole of adolescence ego forces and id forces struggle with each other for the upper hand, a combat which is responsible for many of the conflicting and abnormal manifestations of that period. It is impossible to predict before adolescence is over, whether the individual will emerge from this struggle with a strong or with a weak ego, but this uncertainty is normal and necessary. It is essential for the development of a rich and vivid personality that this part of character formation (the establishment of a definite proportion between id strength and ego strength) should not be terminated too early. The changing flow of libidinal development should, while it lasts, find scope for at least transitory expression without being too crippled by the dictates of a strong ego. On the other hand every new gain in the ego achievements should contribute something towards altering the balance between ego and id and mark a further step in perfecting a sensible management of the instincts.[1] The personality of the child will develop so long as the relationship between ego and id remains fluid and changeable.

The incidence of an infantile neurosis acts like a calcification in the middle of a living organism. Every neurotic symptom represents an attempt at establishing an artificial balance between an instinctive wish and the repressive forces of the ego, a balance which is rigid and, once established, not open to correction. If symptoms multiply and the neurosis organises itself into a coherent structure, the whole relationship between ego and id becomes hopelessly paralysed.

Another and more direct manner in which infantile neuroses reduce ego strength is due to the regression which occurs invariably at the beginning of symptom formation. Libidinal regression is always accompanied by a certain amount of ego regression; ego strength is to a degree dependent on the phase of libido development. The oral organisation of the libido, for instance, always goes together with a special urgency of wishes and impatience for wishfulfilment. That means, practically speaking, that a child who regresses from the genital to the oral level simultaneously regresses from ego strength to ego weakness. Or, to put it differently, regression from the genital to the oral level implies regression from the reality principle to the pleasure principle.

The neurotic child may thus, at first glance, appear to possess a strong ego. But this appearance is misleading. Its ego is committed to a definite and not reversible attitude to an instinct, in order to maintain the delicate balance which is necessary for symptom formation. But its ego is in reality weaker than that of a normal child

[1] A little girl of four and a half, when asked to behave and control herself specially on a certain occasion in the absence of her nurse, answered sensibly, "I think I can manage."

since the id forces have gained a more or less lasting victory in the disguise of symptom formation.

(b) *The qualitative factor in ego-development*

From the first months of life onward the ego develops from a mere meeting point for dimly perceived stimuli into an organised centre where impressions are received, sorted out, recorded, interpreted, and action is taken on the strength of them. (A separate part of the ego fulfils the task of supervising thoughts and actions from a moral point of view [super-ego].) The essential ego functions in this respect are: *testing of inner and outer reality; building up of memory; the synthetic function of the ego;* and *ego control of motility.* All through childhood a ripening process is at work which, in the service of an increasingly better knowledge of and adaptation to reality, aims at perfecting these functions, at rendering them more and more objective and independent of the emotions until they can become as accurate and reliable as any non-human mechanical apparatus. In the last resort, an individual's efficiency in life (under less civilised conditions his chance of survival) is determined by the perfection or imperfection of these ego functions.

But simultaneously with this maturing process another, even more powerful, tendency is at work in the child. These ego achievements are wholly acceptable to it so far as they serve instinct gratification and provide some mastery over the environment. But it soon becomes evident that this new way of functioning brings at least an equal, if not an overwhelmingly greater amount of pain, discomfort and anxiety. Each one of the new functions has its disagreeable consequences. The faithful testing and recording of outside reality reveals to the ego the existence of countless alarming possibilities; the outer world is shown to be full of frustrations, disappointments, threats. The testing of the child's own inner reality reveals the existence of forbidden and dangerous tendencies which offend the child's conception of itself and therefore cause anxiety. The sorting out and interpreting of stimuli, as they arrive, leads to drawing a sharp line of distinction between the child's own self and the objects outside; before this faculty had been developed, the infant had been able to feel itself as one with the world around, to count as itself whatever was pleasurable, and to ascribe to an "outside" what was displeasing. The development of the function of memory is equally disturbing, since it aims at retaining memory traces irrespective of their quality; the infant used to give preference to pleasant memories and to reject the painful ones. The synthetic function of the ego which aims at unifying and centralising all mental processes, is opposed to the free and easy manner in which the infant used to live out its most divergent emotions and instinctive urges either simultaneously or alternately, as for instance love its parents, and hate them, be a passive baby in need of comfort from its mother at one moment, only to confront her as an active male lover and protector the next moment; to destroy possessions, and then immediately afterwards violently to desire and to treasure them. Lastly, a strict ego control of motility permanently deprives the instinctive forces in the id of their former free expression.

Strictly objective functioning of this nature heightens the feeling of tension and anxiety for the ego. On the one side the libidinal forces in the id, represented by the component instincts of infantile sexuality, are felt to clamour for satisfaction. On the other, the adults in the outside world are perceived to threaten punishment or loss of love if the child should indulge in forbidden sexual or aggressive wishes and actions. From the side of the super-ego, i.e. from within, the ego is flooded with feelings of guilt and self criticism whenever it fails to live up to its own standards.

The weak and immature ego of the child fails to stand up to the impact of these dangers. It consequently attempts to undo its own achievements as fast as they are made. It tries not to see outside reality as it is (*Denial*); not to record and make conscious the representatives of the inner urges as they are sent up from the id (*Repression*); it overlays unwelcome urges with their opposites (*Reaction-Formation*); it substitutes for painful facts pleasurable fantasies (escape into *Fantasy-Life*); it attributes to others the qualities which it does not like to see in itself (*Projection*); and it appropriates from them what seems welcome (*Introjection*), etc.

Normally, in every childhood, these methods are used in a moderate degree to defend the ego against anxiety. A certain retrograde movement in the development of the ego achievements is therefore the rule. It does no more than create a certain amount of subjective and faulty functioning which is usually overcome with the beginning of the latency period when the position of the ego is strengthened and anxiety lessens.

But events shape themselves differently where acute neurotic conflicts intervene either in the preoedipal phases or during the Oedipus phase. In the face of excessive anxiety the ego makes excessive and more lasting use of the defence mechanisms at its disposal. Therefore the harm done to the ego functions becomes considerably greater and is of more permanent importance.

Examples of the excessive use of the method of *denial of outside reality* can be found when the child is confronted with the facts of difference of the sexes, which give rise to penis envy and castration anxiety. Under the pressure of these painful emotions the ego waives *reality testing,* pretends to see what is not there (for instance a penis on the mother), or ignores what is in plain view. (A little girl, on watching her new born brother's penis, said, with satisfaction, to her sister: "He has a belly-button just like us," thus remarking on their similarity instead of admitting the obvious difference between them.) Denial makes still greater inroads on reality testing where the central subject of observation of parental intercourse is concerned. Under the influence of their oedipal jealousy children will refuse to realise that their parents have a sex life with each other, and will uphold this denial in spite of all other advances in knowledge of biological facts, of propagation among animals, and even of the facts of life where they concern strangers. Evidence of such denial can be found in countless fairy tales, myths, religious beliefs, etc. Under neurotic conditions it frequently outlives the latency period and adolescence and continues into adult life. But even normally, so long as children avoid admitting reality in this all important respect, they are not free to use their full intelligence for becoming acquainted with outside reality. (An adult neurotic, by profession a medical man, began his analytic cure with the following words: "My parents never had anything to do with each other." Since he was a child in an interminable row of brothers and sisters, there was evidently no truth in his statement. But it contained the key to his neurotic and bizarre behaviour which, to a degree, made his dealings with the real world unpredictable and unreliable.)

Examples of excessive use of the method of *repression* are, by now, common knowledge. Repression occurs invariably when a young child finds itself faced with the intolerable frustration of the component instincts of his early instinctive life. It is easier for the child to stand the clamouring for satisfaction which comes from the id when the representatives of the instincts are refused admittance into consciousness, i.e. are repressed. Since all instinctive manifestations are interrelated, such repression draws ever widening circles until ego and id become entirely estranged from each other. What the neurotic child knows about its own inner life is frequently negligible, at best it is scanty and faulty. *Awareness of inner reality* cannot be upheld under these conditions.

The most instructive instance of neurotic defence doing harm to an ego function is the complete obliteration of childhood memories due to repression. To uphold belief in the asexuality of the parents, or to blot out coitus observations, or scenes of seduction, etc., the memory traces of whole periods of life are removed from consciousness, thus damaging the objectivity of the function of memory, and disrupting and disconnecting the individual's relationship to his own past. Normally all children remove the traces of their earliest years in this manner, to spare themselves the memory of their primitively aggressive, and crudely sexual infantile reactions; but this infantile *amnesia* should not cover more than the first years of life. (A neurotic young girl was able to remember most of her past childhood, with the exception of two years during the latency period, the memory traces of which were completely absent. Her analysis revealed that during this period her widowed mother had been "unfaithful" to her dead father, a fact which the child was trying to ignore.)

Excessive use of *projection* is usually made by neurotic children when dealing with their hostile feelings against father or mother. They either ascribe these tendencies to the parents themselves, or to another child, or to an animal, etc. When used in a normal degree this defence method is an important transitory help in the development of the personality. Used excessively it once more blurs the newly-made distinction between the child itself and the world outside. (A child of two and a half was subject to violent tempers directed against her mother substitute, would shout, throw things at her, etc. When she began to make attempts to overcome these tantrums, she suddenly got hold of the push horse of the nursery, rushed it against the nurse, shouting: "Naughty Jane, jiji bite you now." When the nurse said: "Oh, no, the horse will not bite me, it is not cross with me, but you are," the child laughed and said: "No, me not cross, only jiji." Similarly children ascribe their bad feelings to the "big bad wolf," or some other outside agency, with the result that they themselves can feel all "good" and loving.

Another defence method for dealing with the negative side of the child's ambivalence against the parents is the *splitting of the personality,* with the resulting damage for the *synthetic function* of the ego. For certain periods many children go so far as inventing special names for their "good" and their "bad" selves, though normally they retain the knowledge that both, the good and the bad child are themselves, with a vague feeling of responsibility remaining for both. In an outstanding case of this kind, a girl of six used to refer to her bad side consistently as "the devil" and had ceased to feel any conscious responsibility for the devil's thoughts or actions.

One of the most important advances in ego development during early childhood is the *control of actions* by the ego itself. This is withdrawn when too many actions become invested with symbolical sexual or aggressive significance. The ego then tries first to inhibit them and if unsuccessful, withdraws from certain forms of activity altogether, leaving the control of motility in these respects to the forces of the id. The child then presents a picture, partly of *inhibitions,* partly of unreliable, unpredictable, functioning which is not adapted to reality. (A little girl of three was hardly able to use her hands for any sensible occupation. She used to stretch them out in front of her, lifted up as if warding off actions, her fingers spread wide apart. In this manner she kept herself from committing the aggressions against her little companions with which her mind was constantly occupied in fantasy. —Many boys are greatly disturbed in their urinary function by guilt feelings which arise when they have to touch their genital. They withdraw from this function because for them it implies the wish to masturbate.—A boy of eight was unable to use a knife at table, since he had the fantasy of cutting his mother with it; but withdrawing from this action was of little help since his aggressive wishes dominated other activities, for instance when he was holding a stick, etc., which then from sensible actions suddenly changed into passionate attacks on his mother, etc.)

The common *escape into fantasy* which is of the greatest help to every child, is used excessively under the pressure of neurotic conflicts, and can then become the basis for a complete withdrawal and estrangement from the real world and its demands.

This interference with the ego functions is of greater importance in childhood than it will be, under otherwise similar conditions, in the adult neurosis. It occurs while the ripening process of the ego is still in action. The function which is most directly attacked by the infantile neurosis will, at least temporarily, be kept back from further development, while the other ego achievements continue to mature. Accordingly ego development will become onesided and unharmonious.

The particular defence mechanism which will be most in use, and the particular ego damage which will occur as its consequence, depends on the type of infantile neurosis concerned. In the various forms of hysterical neurosis anxiety is warded off with the predominant help of repression. This may account for the fact that children of the hysterical type, frequently possess a faulty and unreliable memory with consequent difficulties in studying; damage to the function of memory has spread further than the emotionally dangerous memories with which the ego tried to interfere. Obsessional children usually have an excellent and undisturbed memory; but, owing to the excessive ego interference with the free expression of their anal-sadistic tendencies, they are estranged from their own emotions, and are considered cold and unresponsive, even where other than these primitive aggressive-sexual manifestations are concerned. Phobic children deal with their anxieties by withdrawal from their danger-points. They tend to withdraw from many forms of activity altogether and give up motility, far beyond the original range of neurotic danger. As a consequence they frequently become altogether retiring and clumsy in their actions, with passionate and unpredictable outbreaks whenever the motility is governed by the id forces instead of the ego.

With this point of view in mind, it may be possible to assess the seriousness of an infantile neurosis, and with it the need for treatment, in an indirect way, through the harm done to the ego functions by the extensive use of one or several of the neurotic defence mechanisms. There is no reason for alarm or interference when one or another of the ego achievements are reduced, or retarded in their development, or temporarily put out of action. This is a normal and inevitable occurrence. But such retardations may become lasting; several, or all, of the important ego functions may be severely attacked at the same time. If a child shows a faulty knowledge of the outer world, far below the level of its intelligence, if it is seriously estranged from its own emotions; with blank spaces in the remembrance of its own past, beyond the usual range of infantile amnesia; with a split in its personality; and with motility out of ego control; then there can be little doubt that the neurosis is severe, and that it is high time to take therapeutic action.

CONCLUSION

In the foregoing pages an attempt is made to find indications for the therapeutic use of child analysis not so much in the neurotic manifestations themselves, as in the bearing of these manifestations on the ripening processes within the individual child. Emphasis is shifted thereby from the purely clinical aspects of a case to the developmental aspect.

When diagnosing cases from this point of view, the child analyst, or child psychiatrist, has to be as intimately familiar with the normal sequence of child de-

velopment as he is familiar with the neurotic or psychotic disturbances of it. He is, really, faced with the task
of judging the normality of the developmental process
itself.

It is an open question how much help diagnosis of this
kind can receive from academic psychology. The various
mental tests, so far devised, assess circumscribed aspects
of ego development; they are nearly indispensable in
cases where a differential diagnosis between mental
defectiveness and defective awareness of reality through
excessive denial has to be made. The Rohrschach test
goes further into inquiring into the state of libido development and its disturbances. Other tests try to disclose the fantasy life of the individual. It is to be expected that in time further mechanised methods will be
devised to cover an increasingly wider range of the
factors on which a satisfactory diagnosis of infantile neuroses can be based.

At present our analytical knowledge about the developmental processes on the libido as well as on the ego
side is still very incomplete in itself. Besides, too little
is known about the interactions between them, beyond
the fact that a precocious ego is especially intolerant
when coupled with the primitive pregenital component
instincts. We are only slowly learning to distinguish the
various characteristics which mark a neurotic disturbance as either transitory or as permanent, although this
distinction is of extreme importance for our diagnoses.
Not enough is known about the relation between the
development of the purely intellectual factors and the
other important functions of the ego, etc.

Until these gaps are filled by more clinical data from
the psychoanalytical investigation of single children, it
will be necessary not to confine examinations to short-
cuts of any kind, helpful as they may be in furnishing
additional data, but to adhere to the former, lengthy,
laborious, and groping methods of individual approach.

BIBLIOGRAPHY

Abbreviations

Psa.Q.   *The Psychoanalytic Quarterly*, New York.
J.Psa.   *International Journal of Psycho-Analysis.*
Z.Psa.   *Internationale Zeitschrift fuer Psychoanalyse.*
Z.psa.P.   *Zeitschrift fuer psychoanalytische Paedagogik.*
A.J.Orthops. *American Journal of Orthopsychiatry.*
Psa.R.   *Psychoanalytic Review.*

(1) Anna Freud, "Einfuehrung in die Technik der Kinderanalyse," Internat. Psychoanalyt. Verlag, Vienna, 1927.
(2) ———, "On the Theory of the Analysis of Children," *J.Psa.*, X, 1929.
(3) "The Psychoanalytic Study of the Child," an Annual Vol., I, New York, and Imago Publ. Co., London, 1946.
(4) Anna Freud, "Introduction to the Technique of Child-Analysis," Nervous and Mental Disease Monograph Series No. 48, 1929.
(5) Melanie Klein, "The Psycho-Analysis of Children," The Internat. Psycho-Analytical Library, No. 22, 1932.
(6) "Symposion on Child-Analysis," *J.Psa.*, VIII, 1927.
(7) Berta Bornstein, "Zur Psychogenese der Pseudodebilitaet," *Z.Psa.*, XVI, 1930.
(8) ———, "Beziehung zwischen Sexual- und Intellektentwicklung," *Z.psa.P.*, IV, 1930.
(9) ———, "Enuresis und Kleptomanie als passageres Symptom," *Z.psa.P.*, VIII, 1934.
(10) ———, "Phobia in a Two-and-a-half year-old Child," *Psa.Q.*, IV, 1935.
(11) ———, "Leugnung durch die Phantasie," *Z.psa.P.*, X, 1936.
(12) Steff Bornstein, "Eine Technik der Kinderanalyse bei Kindern mit Lernhemmungen," *Z.psa.P.*, VIII, 1934.
(13) ———, "A Child Analysis," *Psa.Q.*, IV, 1935.
(14) Dorothy Burlingham, "Child Analysis and the Mother," *Psa.Q.*, IV, 1935.
(15) ———, "Phantasie und Wirklichkeit in einer Kinderanalyse," *Z.Psa.*, XXIV, 1939.
(16) Edith Buxbaum, "Exhibitionistic Onanism in a Ten-year-old Boy," *Psa.Q.*, IV, 1935.
(17) ———, "The Role of Detective Stories in a Child Analysis," *Psa.Q.*, X, 1941.
(18) Margaret E. Fries, "Play Technique in the Analysis of Young Children," *Psa.R.*, XXIV, 1932.
(19) Elizabeth R. Geleerd, "The Analysis of a Case of Compulsive Masturbation in a Child," *Psa.Q.*, XII, 1943.
(20) Wilhelm Hoffer, "Bericht ueber die Einleitung einer Kinderanalyse," *Z.psa.P.*, IX, 1935.

(21) Anny Katan-Angel, "From the Analysis of a Bed-Wetter," *Psa.Q.*, IV, 1935.

(22) Marianne Kris, "Ein Maerchenstoff in einer Kinderanalyse," *Z.psa.P.*, VI, 1932.

(23) Estelle Levy, "Psychoanalytic Treatment of a Child with a Stealing Compulsion," *A.J.Orthops.*, IV, 1934.

(24) Kata Levy, "Vom Bettnaessen des Kindes," *Z.psa.P.*, VIII, 1934.

(25) Anna Maenchen, "Denkhemmung und Aggression," *Z.psa.P.*, X, 1936.

(26) Editha Sterba, "An Abnormal Child," *Psa.Q.*, V, 1936.

(27) ———, "Excerpt from the Analysis of a Dog Phobia," *Psa.Q.*, IV, 1935.

(28) ———, "Aus der Analyse eines Zweijaehrigen," *Z.psa.P.*, VIII, 1934.

(29) ———, "Ein Fall von Esstoerung," *Z.psa.P.*, IX, 1935.

(30) Jenny Waelder, "Analyse eines Falles von Pavor Nocturnus," *Z.psa.P.*, IX, 1935.

(31) August Aichhorn, "Wayward Youth," Putnam, London, 1936.

(32) ———, "Erziehungsberatung," *Z.psa.P.*, VI, 1932.

(33) ———, "Zur Technik der Erziehungsberatung," *Z.psa.P.*, X, 1936.

(34) ———, "The Juvenile Court: Is it a Solution?" Revue internationale de l'Enfant, Vol. IX, No. 51, March, 1930.

(35) Alice Balint, "Die Psychoanalyse des Kinderzimmers," *Z.psa.P.*, VI, 1932.

(36) ———, "Versagen und Gewaehren in der Erziehung," *Z.psa.P.*, X, 1936.

(37) ———, "Die Grundlagen unseres Erziehungssystems," *Z.psa.P.*, XI, 1937.

(38) Th. Bergmann, "Versuchder Behebung einer Erziehungsschwierigkeit," *Z.psa.P.*, XI, 1937.

(39) Siegfried Bernfeld, "Kinderheim Baumgarten," Juedischer Verlag, Berlin, 1922.

(40) ———, "Sisyphos oder die Grenzen der Erziehung," Internat. Psychoanalyt. Verlag, Vienna. 1925.

(41) ———, "Psychology of the Infant," Kegan Paul, London, 1929.

(42) ———, "Ueber die einfache maennliche Pubertaet," *Z.psa.P.*, IX, 1935.

(43) Steff Bornstein, "Missverstaendnisse in der psychoanalytischen Paedagogik," *Z.psa.P.*, XI, 1937.

(44) Edith Braun, "Eine Kinderfreundschaft. Boebachtung aus einem Kindergarten," *Z.psa.P.*, X, 1936.

(45) Marie H. Briehl, "Die Rolle des Maerchens in der Kleinkindererziehung," *Z.psa.P.*, XI, 1937.

(46) Dorothy Burlingham, "Probleme des psychoanalytischen Erziehers," *Z.psa.P.*, XI, 1937.

(47) Edith Buxbaum, "Massenpsychologie und Schule," *Z.psa.P.*, X, 1936.

(48) H. Fischer, "Sehnsucht und Selbstbefriedigung," *Z.psa.P.*, VII, 1933.

(49) H. Fischer and Lilie Peller, "Eingewoehnungsschwierigkeiten im Kindergarten," *Z.psa.P.*, VIII, 1934.

(50) Anna Freud, "Introduction to Psycho-Analysis for Teachers," George Allen & Unwin, Ltd., London, 1931.

(51) Herta Fuchs, "Psychoanalytische Heilpaedagogik im Kindergarten," Z.psa.P., VI, 1932.

(52) ———, "Probleme der heilpaedagogischen Kindergartengruppen," Z.psa.P., VII, 1933.

(53) Erik Homburger, "Psychoanalysis and the Future of Education," Psa.Q., IV, 1935.

(54) Alice Landau, "Angsterlebnisse eines Dreijaehrigen," Z.psa.P., X, 1936.

(55) Emmi Minor-Zaruba, "Die fuenfjaehrige Nora im Kindergarten," Z.psa.P., XI, 1937.

(56) K. Pensimus, "A Rejected Child," Psa.Q., IV, 1935.

(57) ———, "Folgen der Entrechtung," Z.psa.P., VII, 1933.

(58) Emma Plank-Spira, "Eine Einschlafstoerung aus Todesangst," Z.psa.P., XI, 1937.

(59) Anni Poertl, "Profound Disturbances in the Nutritional and Excretory Habits of a Four and One-half Year Old Boy: Their Analytic Treatment in a School Setting," Psa.Q., IV, 1935.

(60) ———, "Verspaetete Reinlichkeitsgewoehnung," Z.psa.P., VII, 1933.

(61) Fritz Redl, "Zum Begriff der 'Lernstoerung,'" Z.psa.P., VIII, 1934.

(62) ———, "Gedanken ueber die Wirkung einer Phimoseoperation," Z.psa.P., VIII, 1934.

(63) ———, "Der Mechanismus der Strafwirkung," Z.psa.P., IX, 1935.

(64) M. Schmaus, "Bravheit und neurotische Hemmung," Z.psa.P., VII, 1933.

(65) ———, "Esstoerung und Verstimmung," Z.psa.P., X, 1936.

(66) Editha Sterba, "Verbot und Aufforderung," Z.psa.P., VIII, 1934.

(67) ———, "Zwei Arten der Abwehr," Z.psa.P., X, 1936.

(68) ———, "Schule und Erziehungsberatung," Z.psa.P., X, 1936.

(69) Dorothy Burlingham and Anna Freud, "Young Children in War-Time," George Allen & Unwin, Ltd., for the New Era, London, 1942.

(70) ———, "Infants without Families," George Allen & Unwin, Ltd., London, 1943.

(71) Anna Freud, "The Ego and the Mechanisms of Defence," The International Psycho-Analytical Library, No. 30, London, 1937, original German edition, 1936.

(72) Berta Bornstein, "Clinical Notes on Child Analysis," The Psycho-Analytic Study of the Child, Vol. I, New York, 1945, London, 1946.

(73) N. W. Wulff, "Phobie bei einem anderthalbjaehrigen Kinde," Z.Psa., XIII, 1927.

(74) S. Freud, "Analysis of a Phobia in a Five-Year-Old Boy," Collected Papers, III, Hogarth Press, London.

(75) ———, "Three Contributions to the Theory of Sex," Nervous and Mental Disease Monograph Series 7.